# The Heartbeat of Speech-Language Pathology

## Changing the World One Session at a Time

Phuong Lien Palafox, M.S., CCC-SLP
Bilinguistics, Inc.

Published by Bilinguistics, Inc.

For more information, contact Bilinguistics, Inc. or visit us at: www.bilinguistics.com.



ISBN-13: 978-0-578-48862-2
ISBN-10: 0-578-48862-0

This book is dedicated to my mother.

You carried me from sea to land, and your efforts, Má, endlessly inspire our sacred paths.

# A Note from Phuong

*If we are talking technicalities, this book is about the field of speech-language pathology. If you dissect the guts of my work, you will quickly see that our meaningful efforts transcend the boundaries of speech sound production, receptive and expressive language, social-pragmatic skills, voice, and fluency. And with all dissections, both physical and emotional, the work can be overwhelming, hard-won and ultimately, worthwhile.*

*After a decade and a half of working with students in the schools, clients in the clinic, families in their homes, graduate students, speech-language pathology interns, and speech-language pathologists (SLPs) across the nation, here is what I wholeheartedly feel: our work is about people. The foundation and magic of our labor boil down to the humans we serve and the connections we make.*

*Do I believe in evidence-based practices? Absolutely. That being said, I will be the first to say, scream, shout that the research speaks to only one part of our work. The remaining essential parts have to do with the human components: building rapport, earning trust, and loving hard. I am happy to have a civil and passionate conversation with anyone who refutes the importance of the human connection.*

*Progress is made when relationships are created, and the status quo remains when we solely tackle the work without the heart. So, lovely SLPs, the words splattered on these pages are meant to be read* ***and*** *felt. They were written with your exhaustive efforts in mind. You will gain functional, research-based content that you can immediately use, and you will remember why you chose to be a speech-language pathologist in the first place.*

*Here's to our important work, dear friends. We are surely changing the world.*

*With so much love,*

Phuong

# Table of Contents


Prologue 1
- Why This Book? 3
- How This Book Works 5
- Colorful Us 7

Chapter 1. Your SLP Why 9
- The Why. 9
- What it Takes to be A Speech-Language Pathologist. 10

Chapter 2. Evidence-Based Practice 19
- What is Evidence-Based Practice? 19
- Part I: The Research 20
- Part II: SLP Professional Expertise 22
- Part III: Patient/Client/Student/Family Perspective 25

Chapter 3. Lessons for ~~the Beginning of~~ Your Career 29
- For Grief's Sake 29
- A Letter to My Younger SLP-Self: 33
- Lessons Learned 36

Chapter 4. Effective Strategies for All Sessions 39
- The Research 40
- Know Your Goals 46
- Brain-Based Teaching and Learning 48
- Strategies for Brain Engagement 52
- Literacy-Based Interventions 54
- The Big Four: Brain, Heart, Effort, FUN. 60
- The Human I Support 62

Chapter 5. Family Centered Practice 67
- My Family 67

John's Family 69
Research on Family-Centered Practice 71
Chapter 6. Serving our Diverse Populations 89
Valentine 101 89
Spectrum of Diversity 91
Understanding Privilege, Equality and Equity 92
Being Bilingual 94
Language of Kindness 99
What's in a Name? Everything, SLPs. 103
Tips for Remembering Names 104
Moving Forward 105
Gratitude 107
Chapter 7. I See You, SLPs 111
Ode to School-Based SLPs 112
Speech Therapy and Work-Life Balance 118
Be all of YOU in both arenas 122
Epilogue 127
My Heart Honors 131
References 135

# Prologue

Before we dive in, I need to tell you my favorite story. My parents were boat people from Vietnam. My father, Bá, a naval captain for South Vietnam, was imprisoned following the war. After two years, he was released, and he and my mother married. He then navigated a wooden boat to free land for my mother and 54 additional people. Each person was given entry to the treacherous seas by the Vietcong with a bribe of 10 ounces of gold.

On the second day of the journey, the engine died. So Bá hung sheets to catch the wind. On the fifth day, the boat almost capsized due to a heavy storm. On the eleventh day, they arrived in Hong Kong's harbor. I made the journey with ease, as my mother's womb kept me safe during the 11-day journey—only to enter the world at 3am, just hours after their arrival on land. We were lucky. According to the United Nations High Commission for Refugees, between 200,000 and 400,000 boat people died at sea. My parents and I made it.

Within the year, my parents headed to the United States of America. After a year in Whitewater, Wisconsin, our family headed south to Texas and our family eventually relocated to rural Wylie, Texas. As the eldest of three, I was the first to go to school. No one else looked like me in Wylie.

English was foreign on my tongue. So I did not speak. With time, I learned to live in two worlds. My English improved. I became my parents' interpreter and translator, and I assimilated.

My beloved home in Wylie, Texas

This story serves as the foundation of everything I do personally and professionally. My parents' efforts have granted me opportunities that exceeded their initial quiet whisperings of HOPE. They simply wanted to provide a better life for their children. My experience living in a bicultural world and two bedroom home on wheels, with its woes and privilege, laid the foundation for my work supporting the intricate and comprehensive needs of the diverse populations we serve as SLPs.

This is my story, and I share these experiences with a deep fervor for our profession, utmost respect for my peers, and deep love for the individuals I am honored to serve.

## Why This Book?

I have already prefaced that relationships are key in our work, and the crux of this is trust. Some of you have attended my presentations at various state conferences or the American Speech-Language-Hearing Association (ASHA) Conventions. This is part of my work. The main focus of my effort is the caseloads that I have always maintained. At this time, I have clients in our Bilinguistics clinic, I just completed a three-month tenure at a middle school in East Austin, and I support an elementary school whose SLP is on maternity leave for the next five months with a caseload of 28 students across 2.5 days per week. So, dear SLPs, I understand all of it—the hard, the awesome, the effort, the wins, and the daily SLP-grrrrrriiiiinnnnnddddd.

My professional path and time in the trenches have been unique. I have lived these lives, and the perspectives gained in each setting have contributed to the meaningful content of this book. Let's take a walk down my speechy memory lane:

1996 Earned an 1160 on my SAT
2001 Obtained a B.S. from the University of Texas -- Austin, Summa Cum Laude
2002 Was told I was a poor writer because English was not my first language by a clinical supervisor

2002 Conducted research efforts alongside Dr. Jon F. Miller (language guru and creator of S.A.L.T.)

2003 Obtained a M.S. from the University of Wisconsin – Madison

2003 Began my Ph.D. under the leadership of Dr. Ron Gillam and met my future Bilinguistics colleagues, Dr. Ellen Kester and Scott Prath

2003 Discontinued my Ph.D., then found out my mother's cancer had returned the following week

2004 Moved home to Wylie, TX to begin my internship year and support my mother

2004 Worked at the Collin County Special Education Cooperative and was the sole SLP for the Anna Independent School District. Ran the inaugural year of the Language Expansion and Articulation Program (LEAP) at Cox Elementary providing an intensive preschool program for children with needs in the arena of phonological processes and expressive language

2004 My mother passed away during my internship year

2005 Began working for the Round Rock Independent School District (RRISD) and served Laurel Mountain, Purple Sage, Jollyville, and Wells Branch Elementary Schools.

2010 SLP Co-Lead for approximately 50 SLPs for RRISD

2012 Education Specialist for Region 13 Education Service Center – supporting the 60 school districts, charter schools, and private schools in Central Texas

2013 Arrived at Bilinguistics -- SLP in the clinic, schools, and homes. SLP for preschoolers, elementary schools, secondary schools, and adults. SLP in rural school districts, urban school districts, affluent schools, and Title 1 schools.

I am lucky. I have seen a lot as an SLP, all of which has led up to this book. My gestalt perspective shows me common problems across all settings and in all states. Your responses to my writing on The Speech Therapy Blog and for ASHA and after conferences in person have also given me insight. I am witness to the stories you tell me about your successful students. The considerations and ideas shared here are the cumulative efforts of my wide-ranging SLP path and your input these last two decades, SLPs.

## How This Book Works

Now if there is one thing I know about SLPs, it's that we like to know the schedule. Expectations are crucial for our sanity and productivity. I get it. . . because I, too, have self-preservation needs. There is no satisfaction like creating a list and intently crossing off a completed action item. Write book for SLPs. Check! So I want to lay out an expectation. Brené Brown (2018), a gifted researcher on the topic of vulnerability and courage, tells us, "Clear is kind. Unclear is unkind." And because I believe in kindness, I want you to know that this book will address the skills needed for working your way through an SLP day.

I'll address the evidence-based practices necessary to support your endeavors to make sounds clearer, increase mean length of utterance, improve vocal quality, foster the emotional and fluency needs of people who stutter, and facilitate the social skills of people navigating this complex world. Some of you will read the chapter headings and quickly realize that it is not necessarily the research you find in our professional journals. You are absolutely correct. Give your brain a kiss. Rather, this book will address the human components of our profession. This includes considerations for supporting the emotional and social needs of our clients, tips for mentally and physically organizing your overwhelming day and strategies to navigate common, and difficult SLP scenarios. I want to note that as SLPs, we work with students, clients, and patients. For the sake of brevity in this book, the terms will be used interchangeably.

Along my SLP journey, I have realized that, often, our success is not necessarily *what* we do as speech-language pathologists; it's *how* we go about doing it. And, how you do it, at times, can yield some pretty amazing outcomes for those you serve and awesome-SLP-you.

## Colorful Us

One more thing before we dive into the chunky content. The work I do serves humans from all cognitive, linguistic, cultural and socio-economic backgrounds. That being said, my effort and heart focus on our most vulnerable populations. At Bilinguistics, we specialize in supporting our diverse communities. We do this because the demographics of our nation have diversified (U.S., Census, 2018), and as SLPs we are serving these individuals. We do this because the research on assessment and intervention of our diverse populations trails behind the research on native English speakers. We do this because there are unique and important considerations when supporting students and clients of color with communication needs, those exposed to two or more languages, individuals from different religious backgrounds, and members of the LGBTQ+ communities.

This book was written to support your efforts to serve the needs of your diverse caseloads. Know what's awesome? As speech-language pathologists, we are already good at differentiation and scaffolding. It's what we do. We will apply these techniques broadly to connect with those we serve and positively impact their lives. Here's to your work and to honoring the individualized narrative of each person you serve.

# Chapter 1. Your SLP Why

*I want to empower people. I want to be a speech-language pathologist.*

The Why.

This book has been written in my head and heart for years, and I have always known that this would be the first chapter. What is your why? Each of us has our own unique answer to this question. Simon Senek (2017) describes this as the purpose, cause, or belief that inspires you to do what you do. Why did you get into this field in the first place? For me, my closest childhood friend was a person who stuttered. I remember him changing his order at restaurants to avoid stuttering on a word. At times, I would sit across from him knowing that he was eating something he did not enjoy. We rehearsed his high school presentations late into the evening. It was the catalyst to my profession, and I am grateful for that gift. So, my *why* is that, at the end of the day, I help human hearts feel better by helping them tell their stories.

I know that the work we do in our field is not easy. In fact, there are days when you guys tell me that you want to quit. *I have too many on my caseload. I have no idea how to test a person who is non-verbal. Am I making a difference?* In those moments, remember your WHY. You tell me that you got into the field to help others. *You surely are.* You tell me you got into the field to support children with autism. *You already have, and your student and his family are thankful for you*. You tell me that your adult client is now able to get a job because of the communication device you helped support. *You were a (BIG) part of his success*. When we are bogged down with the daily paperwork, bureaucracy and documentation, it is easy to dwell in the land of the *what do I do* and *how the heck do I do this*. Take a long breath, and listen to my first/then directive, SLPs.

*First, remember your why.*
*Then, write it down.*
*These words will carry you.*

*My SLP Why*:

________________________________________

________________________________________

________________________________________

## What it Takes to be A Speech-Language Pathologist.

*What's it like to be a speech-language pathologist?* I am often asked this from those considering our roles and responsibilities. Like, whoa, I get overwhelmed thinking about all of the nuances of this complex profession. My answer changes daily. Sometimes, it changes hourly. We are in the thick of it. Evaluations and reports are always due, timelines feel much too short, sweat stains are making repeated appearances, and our human (and SLP) reserves are running low.

### The Good.

You chose to be a speech-language pathologist for an important reason. So, why did you do it? Here is what some SLPs shared. Maria said, "I am a speech pathologist because I want to empower others – so that they can ultimately empower themselves using their words and others' words as tools for their learning and growth." Scott said, "I am energized that I did some good, connected with someone, and pulled them forward." Alisa's SLP why began with her own narrative. "Moving to the U.S. as a child, and growing up in a bilingual/bicultural home, I realized I wanted to use the languages that I know to help children with language disorders and be able to support them in their native tongue." There are many reasons, and they are all honored. Remember chapter one, folks? Know and believe in your SLP Why.

### The Hard.

Here's the thing. These days happen often. There are days when:

*I leave work crying.*
*The paperwork is stacked too high.*

*My student did not make progress.*
*I spend hours in the evening writing a report.*
*I don't feel smart enough.*

Now, here is my confession. I need to apologize to each of you. I often find myself standing in front of you and telling you all that it is going to be okay. You will be okay, SLP, and your efforts are always worth it. You come up to me after presentations, your eyes wet, and tell me that I convinced you not to quit. We hug, and I'm grateful we kept another great SLP in the profession. You email me about your caseload of almost 100 students, and I help you problem-solve how to talk to your district superintendent to get another SLP position. You thank me, and I'm hopeful that you will have a reprieve from some of your daily professional efforts, soon. You write to me and ask if it is worthwhile to switch to the profession of speech-language pathology. I write back and tell you about the meaningful outcomes of my profession, and you tell me that you will work hard to join the SLP ranks. In the last few months, the quiet whisperings of, "This is not right," "How am I supposed to do this?" and, "Is it really worth it?" have been getting resoundingly louder. *So, we need to talk.*

I acknowledge the problems that exist within our field. Last year, I worked in a district alongside an SLP-Intern who was serving almost 90 students across 6 campuses, and I just spoke to an SLP who supports one SLP-Assistant with an anticipated caseload of 100+ for the following school year. I understand the frustrations of getting denied authorization for your client who is a person with Autism Spectrum Disorders (ASD) and is a non-verbal communicator. The real-life scenarios of caseloads I've covered and the whispered confessions of my SLP peers are unexpected and disheartening. And, dearest SLPs, this is not a "people problem." This is not YOU. This is a "systems problem." (Cockerell, 2010)

Remember "being kind" is "being clear." Right now, I want to be VERY clear. We need to make changes to our systems. We need school systems to know the scope of our responsibilities and understand that increased caseloads require additional personnel to ethically fulfill our professional efforts. We need managed care organizations (a.k.a., insurance) to understand the scope of denial of services when authorizations cannot be fulfilled. Let us also acknowledge the productivity requirements in hospitals and skilled nursing facilities and the subsequent documentation and paperwork that is to be completed off the clock. Because our workload has increased, I see you trying to stay afloat.

Examples of these practices include:

- SLPs recommend 30 minutes of therapy weekly because they cannot physically see the students for more time.
- SLPs are compliant on IEP and evaluation deadlines. Therapy minutes

are secondary because it's not tracked by the district or "we can always make-up compensatory minutes later."

- SLPs dismiss students once they get to the secondary level because there are not enough SLPs.
- SLPs do not have time to conduct an evaluation and write up a report to dismiss students. So, they keep and keep and keep staying on the caseload.
- SLPs tell their teachers, "I don't have time. Just pick the worst student in your class."
- SLPs are told they CANNOT recommend more than one 30-minute session per week.
- SLPs do not qualify students.
- SLPs are quitting.

Again, I need my SLPs to wholeheartedly know that I do not blame them for these mishaps. This is the direct result of what has been placed on our very full speechy plates. It is not a "people problem." It is an "exhaustion" problem. You are all tired, and you are barely hanging on. This is not okay. This is not okay. You got it, SLP? You're right. This is very hard, and **this is not okay.**

The Reason.

As I conclude this chapter, I need to bring it back home--this is you, SLP. I have spent the last few months thinking often and deeply of your daily woes. You tell me that you got into this profession to support the communication journeys of your students and their families. Know that you are. It's amazing. As you talk to me about your caseloads, inundations of evaluations and reports and Medicaid billing, you also start sharing your students' success stories. You talk about how he started putting together a sentence. You talk about the creative ways you use science experiments in speech-language therapy. You talk about the scholar that started using her communication board to request her favorite breakfast.

This helps me remember, too. I remember all of those faces. I remember John. I met him when I was in graduate school, and I served him for two years as an Applied Behavior Analysis (ABA) treatment technician. I still keep in touch with his mother, Anne. I remember Jessie. I worked with him for four years on his narrative and conversational skills. In our final session, we talked and laughed about everything and nothing–it was lovely and meaningful. I remember Mary. We worked on her thoughts and feelings about stuttering. When it was time to work on her career project, I expected her to do her research on being a basketball player—she talked about Brittney Griner, a professional basketball player who currently plays for the Phoenix Mercury, endlessly. She shook her head. "What are you going to be then?" I asked. "Y-y-y-you. I w-w-w-wwwant to be y-y-you. I w-w-w-wwwant to emp-p-p-p-power people." She completed her project on becoming a speech-language pathologist.

To be a speech-language pathologist is to make a difference. We make a meaningful difference. So, now, sit back and read my hip-hop lyrics. This was written with SLP-love and admiration. This moment is sponsored by the Letter B. So, SLPs, drop me a B-B-B-Beat. (Credit given to Lupe Fiasco's *Show Goes On*):

For the SLPs

Have you ever had the feeling
That you were meant to be
An advocate for words and thoughts
For kids and families.
With hope all in your soul,
And exhausting college days,
You worked, you read, you wrote
And found your speechy ways.
Then, came that fateful day
With cap and gown in hand
On top of the world
Excitement you withstand
You get your j. o. b.
And start your life's work
The glitter starts to dim,
Paperwork does lurk
Your days are long and hard
For this I surely know
Not 'nuf money in the world
Your worth immeasurable

You show up every day
Support in all the ways
For the work keeps coming always, always,
not fazed.

**Hands in the Air**

One in the air for SLPs here
Two in the air for kids we hold dear
Three in the air for the books we read
Four in the air 'cause we will succeed.
Five in the air for the hope
We hold for the kids we serve
Worth bars of gold
We won't hold them back
And the world is theirs!
Yeah yeah, the world is yours,
I was once that little girl
Terrified of the world;
Now, I live and I am sure:
I will give up everything,
Even fight a dinosaur
For these little girls
And boys I'm rapping round' the world for!
Vietnam to Hong Kong, then I came to the USA,
Teachers, parents believed in me
Listen up. I love my days!

**For the Humans We Serve**

So no matter what you been through
No matter what you into
No matter what you see when you look outside your
window
Brown grass or green grass
Picket fence or barbed wire
Never, ever put them down
You just lift your arms higher
Raise 'em 'til your arms tire
Let em' know you're there
That you struggling and survivin'

That you gonna persevere
Yeah, ain't nobody leavin',
Nobody goin' home
Even if they turn the lights out. The work,
*Our important work,* must go on!

Here's the thing. Despite EVERYTHING that is happening against you, you show up. You show up, and you work hard. If you would like to listen to this, visit: https://www.bilinguistics.com/the-work-must-go-on

# Chapter 2. Evidence-Based Practice

*You hold your own magic. Be you, SLP. Everyone else is already taken.*

During my college days, I spent time thinking about my team's football schedule, listening to the woes of Matchbox 20 and hearing the adamant insistence on using evidence-based practices (EBP) from my professors. Somewhere along the way, the insistence on this practice made me anxious. *Am I using the latest research? Where do I find the time to read research journals? Am I smart enough for all of this?* I would like to revisit the definition of EBP as you begin to read this book. Oftentimes, we only consider the information found in research articles to be EBP. This is only one-third of what we need to consider.

## What is Evidence-Based Practice?

Today, I want to take us back to the basics of EBPs. My gut tells me you're doing more than you think. What does our ASHA mothership say? EPB is comprised of three *equal* parts. EBP is made up of three parts? What?! I know. I know. As you move through this book, think about how the content addresses 1) the scientific research, 2) your professional expertise, and 3) the patient and the family's perspective. The information written within these pages is an homage to **all three** important parts.

## Part I: The Research

We all know about the research part. When I work alongside SLPs who are worried about the research, I see that they are naturally using strategies that are supported by the research: modeling (Griffin, Sam, & AFIRM Team, 2016), imitation and drill procedures for speech sound disorders (Wren, Harding, Goldbart, & Roulstone, 2018), literacy-based interventions (Peterson, 2011), social skills training (Griffin, Sam, & AFIRM Team, 2016), curriculum-based language intervention (Powell, Randolph, & Meaux, 2016), etc. If this part still overwhelms you, I'll give you some helpful and easy-to-use links at the end of this chapter.

Keeping up-to-date on the research in the field can seem daunting. ASHA has done excellent work to facilitate this process for all of us. They provide evidence maps for many different areas, including Apraxia of Speech, Autism Spectrum Disorders, Cerebral Palsy, Cleft Lip and Palate, Speech Sound Disorders, and many other categories. Within each topic, they group the studies by External Scientific Evidence (the vast majority of the articles fall in this category), Clinical Expertise, and Client Perspectives. For each article, a summary of the conclusions from the study is included. *I'll let you in on a secret. It usually takes me 5 minutes or so to scan for my topic and read the conclusions*. You can find the maps at https://www.asha.org/Evidence-Maps/. In the case that you do not have the time to peruse the maps, here is some research that I found useful as a practicing clinician in the schools and in our Bilinguistics clinic:

Fluency:

Consideration for successful fluency outcomes includes interventions that address "emotional/ psychological/social aspects, incorporating 'real-world' elements, having follow-up sessions and interacting with other people who stutter" (Baxter, Johnson, et al., 2016). This means that stuttering therapy needs to move beyond teaching skills needed for fluent speech. Instead, a comprehensive approach that includes "increasing acceptance of stuttering and of being a person who stutters, reducing secondary behaviors, minimizing, avoidance, improving communication skills, increasing self-confidence, managing bullying effectively, and ultimately, minimizing the adverse impact of stuttering on the child's life" (Yaruss, Coleman, & Quesal, 2012) should be implemented.

Language:

Are books magical? Perhaps. Is teaching literacy considered evidence-based? Absolutely. A study by Peterson in 2011 "revealed that narrative intervention with repeated story retellings and a focus on narrative macrostructure may be sufficient to facilitate a significant improvement in both narrative macrostructure and some aspects of narrative microstructure." This means you can use the same book for an entire month to address major story grammar components, and these efforts will improve children's overall ability to understand and tell a story, including the details!

School-Based Considerations:

Collaborating with our teachers and educational assistants is meaningful. Our "educational personnel can successfully implement functional communication skills" (Andzik, Cannella-Malone, et al., 2016). This means that our work, SLPs, cannot exist in a vacuum. Involve your educational peers, please.

## Part II: SLP Professional Expertise

Second, and equally important, is your professional expertise and opinion. What do you bring to the table, SLPs? Your one-third of EBP includes the knowledge you have gained from your educational background, your past experiences as an SLP, and the choices you provide your students, clients, and families based on this knowledge. Remember, without your input, decisions cannot be made regarding assessment and intervention. Value your contributions.

I've walked into a space filled with SLPs, and we are not a shy, quiet group. Yet we start doubting ourselves when we do not know all the answers. Remember, our profession is built on continual learning. If you do not know, it's okay. That's the time to consult our journals, Google Scholar, asha.org and, most importantly, our SLP-peers. If you do not know the answer, I guarantee that there is an SLP who is willing to give his/her expert thoughts and experiences on the matter. As a former speech-language pathologist in RRISD, I had access to a list of my SLP peers' areas of expertise. The list was a compilation of each SLP's favorite topic. So, when I had a fluency evaluation, I looked at my list and called Jean, an SLP expert on the topic. When I had doubts about my skills for Augmentative and Alternative Communication, I reached out to Jenell. My peers kindly offered their SLP brains, and it saved me a great deal of time and effort. I was then able to move forward in areas where I had previously felt stuck.

When you start out in the field, you are implementing therapy as you have been taught. In time, you realize that a single approach does not work for everyone in a single category, say speech sound disorders. You learn to adjust your approach, provide more or less support, provide visual cues, use repetition, use video modeling, add tactile cues, and so on and so forth. You build an instinct for what works and for ways to change things when they do not work. Trust your instinct. It is born from experience and is a critical part of your evidence-based practice. Also know that as you gather more information from your student, changes can be made. An important part of EBP is understanding that we are working with dynamic systems. People change continually, and the ebb and flow of our SLP responses is not only to be expected, but is necessary.

Lastly, I need to talk about the Imposter Syndrome. This is a psychological pattern where you doubt your efforts and your experiences, and you feel that you are about to exposed as a "fraud." I see this within my SLP peers, and I see this within myself. "Sheesh, all of these people think that I know what I'm doing as an SLP! I'm totally getting away with this, but the truth is about to be revealed. I have no idea what I'm doing. I don't even know how to spell disfluency/dysfluency. I'll just write "not fluent" in the report!" If you are one of the SLPs faced with this, take note:

1. **Acknowledge that you feel this way.** It takes power away from it.
2. **Lead with transparency.** It's okay to not have an answer. Acknowledge it, find the answer and get back with an answer. People appreciate the truth and your effort.
3. **Know that you provide value.** We chose to be in a human profession. By default, we provide a valuable service to each human with whom we interact. We connect with them on a human level. It's inevitable.
4. **There is only one YOU.** You are the only Scott/Maritza/Ellen/(fill in your name) that exists with your stories and your skills and your truths, and the world needs you.

You hold your own SLP magic. What is your area of expertise? Do not tell me that you don't have one. I'll wait while you think of a topic that gets you SLP-giddy. Remember, I'm a speech-language pathologist. I'm good at waiting for a response.

*As an SLP, I love talking about*

________________________________________,

*and it's okay to share my knowledge and passion for this topic with my peers.*

## Part III: Patient/Client/Student/Family Perspective

Third and last, we need to consider our patients, clients, students, and their families' perspectives. Recently, I did a keynote for a school district's parent conference. Annually, the school district puts on a free conference for the families of children in special education. Prior to my presentation, I walked around and talked to some of the attendees.

I spoke to a mother and father who received a diagnosis of autism for their 6-year-old daughter. "That sounds hard," I said. The mother continued to speak as tears dripped from her face. "It's been a really hard year for us. I was diagnosed with epilepsy and my mother-in-law passed away this year." I spoke to another woman who has a grown son. He loves movies, and he is also an individual with autism. I said, "Tell me about him." She pragmatically stated that he stays at home, and he was currently at home with his father. Then, I spoke to another mother who has 4 children. She spoke about how her two older children are typically developing, and her two younger children have specialized needs. She reported that both daughters are doing well; however, initially, she was so overwhelmed with what she needed to do to help them.

Each family's story was so very different, and all of the narratives I heard were important. This is where we *listen* and consider what's most valuable to those we serve. Addressing a family's needs can be difficult without having upfront, valuable conversations. I acknowledge that the topics can also be sensitive and personal. In turn, when I initially talk to my families, I say words along the lines of, "Tell me about your biggest worries. Tell me about him. That sounds hard." This is an open-ended comment that allows the family the time and space to give the information they want to share. Remember, more information is shared as more trust is earned, and **we need to earn that trust**.

I remember talking to San Juana, a mother to a young man I was seeing in the clinic. Her son, Christopher, is an individual who loves to draw. Christopher is also a person with Down Syndrome and is a non-verbal communicator. When I asked about her concerns, she mentioned that the family depends on the city's transportation to get to our clinic. This is important to her because I was saying that they needed to come to our office *twice* a week. What would be a 10-minute drive for families with a personal car is, for this family, an endeavor that includes waiting on a city van that arrives within a 2-hour window, waiting for their time therapy slot, speech-language therapy, and, finally, waiting again for the city vehicle to arrive. I acknowledge that there were days when San Juana and Christopher gave up on the van, walked to the closest bus stop and took the bus home. On the hardest of days, they would walk all the way home.

Ultimately, the goal of EBP is to provide communication opportunities to our clients with their functional and individualized needs in mind. A passionate SLP, Allison Long, truthfully and eloquently says, "To think that what happens outside of our sessions doesn't affect us within the walls of our therapy room is pure fallacy." She is right. Stay tuned for Chapter 5. SLPs, in the words of Rob Thomas of Matchbox 20, "**Our [SLP] lives are made in these small hours**." We are doing significant work, and these increments, the 30/45/60-minute sessions *and* the moments spent reaching out to your students and their families add up. You have quick access to the research, you have your experience (it's relevant regardless of the years under your belt), and you have the heart-needs of your patients close to your own heart. **You've got this.**

The remainder of this book will dive a bit deeper into the considerations for the final third component of evidence-based practices. The patient-client-student-family perspective *or family values based on meaningful and individualized experiences*, will be broken down into various parts. I will be talking about how the following topics can impact many family perspectives and values such as cultural needs, socio-economic considerations, family narratives over time and the value of relationships. This will all be considered within the roles and responsibilities of your efforts as a speech-language pathologist. As promised, here are easy-to-navigate sites that provide content for evidence-based practices:

AUTISM EBP

- NATIONAL PROFESSIONAL DEVELOPMENT CENTER ON AUTISM SPECTRUM DISORDERS (NPCD): NPDC USED A RIGOROUS CRITERIA TO CLASSIFY 27 FOCUSED INTERVENTIONS AS EBPS.
- AUTISM INTERNET MODULES (AIM): AIM PROVIDES ONLINE MODULES FOR 24 EVIDENCE-BASED PRACTICES.

LITERACY-BASED EBP

- LITERACY-BASED SPEECH AND LANGUAGE THERAPY ACTIVITIES: THIS TOOL, PRODUCED BY AND AVAILABLE FROM BILINGUISTICS, PROVIDES EBPS FOR USING LITERACY-BASED INTERVENTIONS AND PROVIDES TEMPLATES FOR BOOK-BASED ACTIVITIES FOR AGES 3 TO ADULTHOOD.

EBP PER ASHA

- THIS FOLLOWING SITE OFFERS EBPS FOR LANGUAGE, SPEECH, FLUENCY AND MORE: HTTPS://WWW.ASHA.ORG/RESEARCH/EBP/EBSRS/

# Chapter 3. Lessons for ~~the Beginning of~~ Your Career

*There will be hard days. There will also be days when you are making an impact—it's all the days that you are a speech-language pathologist.*

## For Grief's Sake

It was 2004, and I couldn't do it anymore. I quit my doctoral program, and the next week I found out Má's cancer had returned. The timing was impeccable, and I moved home to be with my mother and start my CF Internship. My days were spent making mistakes, learning, and becoming a professional. My evenings were spent by my mother's side. A majority of our time was filled with shared meals and shared stories. She continued to mother, and I happily obliged her. One weekend, she accompanied me to my campus to help set up my speech room. She found comfort in caring for my classroom needs. Her arms moved with effort as she wiped each surface. Her small, skilled fingers picked up pieces of trash that could have been easily vacuumed. I found the constant and quick slap of her flip flops reassuring as I prepared for my new school and my new space. After that Sunday, Má was a creating-zealot. As a seamstress, her superpower was to create items with careful detail. She made me a grab bag out of discarded rainbow fabric. I used the grab bag following each phonological and literacy lesson, and I was always proud when telling my 3-, 4- and 5-year-old students that my mother made the magical bag. That December, she passed away on a cold morning. I was 26 years old. I'm glad I had that year with Má--she saw me become a speech-language pathologist.

Twelve years later, in 2016, I was asked to supervise Leah Joseph, a Clinical Fellowship Intern. Our relationship was typical for a supervisor and an intern. I observed her sessions and assessments. I recounted her successes and she would share one goal to address for the future. Then, in January of 2017, her mother passed away from complications related to Amyotrophic Lateral Sclerosis (ALS). Leah shared that her mom's life lessons and legacy gave her the strength to continue her journey to become a licensed speech-language pathologist. Because life bestows gifts in the most inexplicable ways, I wholeheartedly understood her sentiments.

When I think back on my career as an SLP, it's hard for me to separate the events of my first year. Our lives as speech-language pathologists are shaped by our narrative, and my mother was surely a main character in my story. Her death, methinks, has been the single most impactful event in my life thus far. For a long time, I pieced apart SLP-Phuong and human-Phuong. I finally realized that the two parts together made up the truest version of myself.

As you navigate your professional responsibilities, I want you to know that life will continue to happen. As clinical professionals, we focus on the needs of our clients and students. We also need to consider our personal needs. Below are considerations for the grieving SLP heart. Leah and I originally shared this content with ASHA in an article titled *Working Through Grief: Two SLPs Share Their Stories.* I know that the topic of loss may not be relevant in your life; however, from where I stand, grief has a tendency to find its way into our lives—the loss of a human, the loss of a dream, the loss of expectations, the loss of your former self.

Take this into consideration as you walk through your journey as a speech-language pathologist:

1. Ask for Help:

Getting help is okay, and, at times, it's the only solution. During her time of crisis, Leah quickly informed others of her absence. A co-worker helped to notify her clients' families. Seek help and then accept it. And, I promise, you'll do your fair share of helping others, too.

2. Be Okay with Taking Time Off:

We both took about a week off. Know that you have just experienced a trauma. A reprieve from work will allow you to process new information, take care of necessary action items, and begin grieving.

3. Grief Does Not End:

Grief is not linear, and there is not an end to it. When it chooses to show up at work, honor your feelings. Find your way to survive the moment. For me, setting aside 20 minutes to actively grieve before the work day helped.

4. Share the Person:

Sharing memories of your loved one is okay. During an initial "check in" for a social skills group, I shared that I missed my mother. One student reached his hand out and said, "It's okay, Ms. Phuong." That authentic moment, coincidentally, also served as a functional opportunity to address socio-emotional goals.

5. You Will Find Joy Again:

A time will come when you will be able to immerse yourself in daily routines—this includes responding to emotions other than sadness. Know that joy and grief can exist in the same space.

This momentous year in 2004, as gut-wrenching as it was, gifted me many lessons. As with many life-things, I was not yet ready to listen. It was not until almost a decade and a half later that I fully understood the scope of my clinical fellow internship. So, as a 40-year-old, I sat down to write a letter to my former self.

## A Letter to My Younger SLP-Self: 5 SLP Lessons

*Dear Phuong,*

*You just walked out of your first graduate school class, and you're on your own in Badger country. You are 22, and I, on the other hand, exist 18 years later as the 40-year-old version of you. You are about to dive into your chosen profession as a speech-language pathologist, and today I am in the thick of it. To the right of me is a four-inch stack of paperwork. To the left of me is a file containing information for a (not yet written) report. And, on this chilly day in Austin, I have thoughts of you. I have 43 minutes before a client walks through the door. So, listen up.*

### Here are 5 SLP lessons:

#### 1. Learn

You don't know what you're doing... yet. With time and experience, it will get easier. Then something new will pop up, and you'll be back at square one feeling unskilled.

Remember, success in this field, as in most, depends on continual learning. Be transparent with what you know, seek out the experts, listen, and learn. Then, when you have the opportunity to be the expert, share your knowledge openly and kindly.

2. Mistakes are Expected

I have yet to meet a colleague who has not made an error. Mistakes are expected, and my internship year is blatant proof of that fact. Oh, the sea of red I used to see on my reports that inaugural year. Here's what you do when this happens: own up to the blunder, find out what to do differently next time, and make it right. The mistake is not what matters most. Rather, it's how you recover and how you treat others (and yourself) along the way.

3. Be Student/Client Centered

You have chosen to put your efforts in a profession that supports fellow humans. This means effective speech-language therapy sessions are built on a foundation of human needs. Sure, you're learning about research, strategies, and data right now. That's only half of the work. You need to honor the whole client. Here's the thing: you will not necessarily learn these skills in school. Instead, seek the professionals who are well-respected and loved. See how they interact with others—honoring the heart, choosing to see strengths in others, finding the solutions? Do the same thing, and follow their lead.

4. Seek Help

I see independent-you. Listen up: getting help is okay, and at times, it's the only solution. In about four years, Phuong, your life will change. Má will pass away during your CF internship year. Many will offer to help, and you will decline. You eventually learn to accept help. A decade later another tragedy strikes. This time, you allow colleagues and friends to support you, and their efforts will astound you. Seek help and then accept it. I promise, you'll do your fair share of helping others, too.

5. You Do YOU

I know that you are constantly telling yourself that you should (fill in skill) just like (fill in name of someone else). There's only one you, and the only book for how you should/could/need to be can only be written by your brain and heart. You are emotional. Use that power to connect with your families. You love hip-hop. Use that passion in your sessions. You love books. Use them as your medium to build communication. When you are comfortable with being the best version of you, I promise that's when everything will align.

That's all the SLP lessons I have for you, Phuong. Okay, many years later you will still be particular with time management. I have three minutes left, and sweet Sammy will walk through the door. And, you know what's going to happen? He will see you and say, "Ms. Phuong! I'm going to find my sounds!" His mother, Nada, will smile. She just called you this week to thank you for your efforts. A year ago, Sammy was working hard to put two words together, and *our* efforts have made a positive difference in his life.

So, dear Phuong, you are about to enter the best profession. Sure, there will be hard days. And there will be days when you are making an impact—it's every day that you are a speech-language pathologist.

## Lessons Learned

I see the value in learning from my own life lessons. I also think it's important to listen to others. In the summer of 2017, after attending ASHA Connect in New Orleans, a conference designed for SLPs in the schools, health care, and private practice, I finally understood the secret of how to be a successful speech-language pathologist. Here's what happened. I, along with 5 fellow SLPs, was given the task of sharing a "big message" to the attendees at the closing conference session. This is *what* we had to do, and I was excited. Then, we were told *how* it was going to happen. We were given exactly 5 minutes and 20 slides. The catch? The slides would automatically advance every 15 seconds. Upon hearing this, I became nauseated. On the other hand, I always like a challenge, and this sounded fun. Just call me Phun-Phuong.

So there I was with sitting alongside Dr. Barbara Ehren (University of Central Florida), Dr. Sandra Gillam (Utah State University), Dr. Ann Kummer (Cincinnati Children's and the University of Cincinnati College of Medicine), Dr. Gregory Lof (MGH Institute of Health Professions) and Dr.

Tommie Robinson, Jr. (Division of Hearing and Speech Children's National Health System). Now, if you all remember from my SLP timeline, I quit my doctoral program. I typically don't live in the Land of Regret. It's wasted energy. However, my thoughts yelled, "You don't have those three letters after your name! YOU DON'T HAVE THOSE THREE LETTERS AFTER YOUR NAME. I just see four letters: Q.U. I. and T." Thankfully, I regained control, and I kindly told my ego to simmer its ridiculousness.

I got to go first (thank goodness), and I spoke about the foundation of our profession–making connections with our students, clients, and families. And the way to connect with others is through stories. I completed my task, and I sat down. It was time to listen to my fellow speakers. I'll be honest. I was intimidated, and I listened closely. These brains were going to share their brilliance, and I was going to take note. Oh, they were outstanding.

Here's the thing, y'all: The takeaway message had nothing to do with speech, language, fluency, voice, or dysphagia. Instead, the general consensus was:

1. Lead with your heart and lead with compassion.
2. Believe in yourself and your efforts.
3. Connect with others through stories.
4. Be nice.
5. Have fun, fun, fun.

The final session concluded, and it was time to go back home to Texas. As I waited for my flight, I reflected. All of the speakers chose to speak about the *human component* of our field. We need to see the heart-value of our peers and clients first. Then, we get to some great speech-language pathology. So, you ask, how can I become a successful SLP? Dear friends, you already are.

# Chapter 4. Effective Strategies for All Sessions

*First, I work on the relationship and gain the trust. Then, we begin our communication journey. These are the foundational tools for a speech-language pathologist.*

I've spent approximately 9,720 hours doing speech-language therapy, and I've discovered a secret to great speech-language therapy sessions. For me, it boils down to five ideas:

1. Relationship & Rapport
2. Know Your Goals
3. Brain-Based Interventions
4. Literacy-Based Interventions
5. Honor Brain, Heart, Effort, & Fun

Evidence-based practices are essential to our success. However, to me, something else supersedes the research and the academic tenets we were taught in graduate school. What is it? To get to the head (speech and language skills), this SLP needs to go through the heart. Say it with me, "To get to the head, you go through the heart." So what does that mean?

The Research

For a long time, I thought I was just emotional—all the time. I cry often, and it is difficult to hide my feelings. Within the last five years, I realized that this is my SLP Superpower. I started to research it. With brain science and social health research on my side, I learned that the lovey-dovey stuff, in reality, is essential to our work as speech-language pathologists.

In 2017, I learned about the work of Dr. Jeffrey Duncan-Andrade. He is the founder of Roses in Concrete Community

School in East Oakland and is an Associate Professor at San Francisco State University specializing in Raza Studies. He believes in providing children with basic needs before they can learn. SLPs, this goes back to our graduate school days and learning about Maslow's Hierarchy. He states, "I've always understood intuitively that Maslow was right: I have to start at food, shelter, clothing, safety, and then I have to create a space that gives them a sense of love and belonging...I know you have to win the heart to win the head. But most of my training and the professional development I'd get was about the head.

I had to leave the field of education and get into conversations in public health and neuroscience and these other fields to understand from a research perspective what I needed to pay attention to. I knew once kids felt safe, the head would open up for me." Duncan-Andrade (2016) tells us that without a positive relationship between a child and his teacher, learning will not take place. He discusses the value of building the relationship to allow learning to happen. In the arena of speech-language pathology, rapport and trust with the student will yield greater outcomes for gains in speech, language, and social-pragmatic skills.

So, SLPs, repeat his words, "Win the heart to win the head." Here's a two-step directive for your speech and language sessions. First, support your students' and clients' heart needs. Then, work on speech and language skills. That's what you need for a great speech therapy session. Here's another way of thinking about it: In Dare to Lead, Brené Brown writes, "Leaders must either invest a reasonable amount of time attending to fears and feelings, or squander an unreasonable amount of time trying to manage ineffective and unproductive behavior." As leaders in our battlefield of speech-language pathology, we need to support our students' and clients' emotional health first. It's okay to spend time on this, and I would say that it's essential before communication skills can be addressed and ultimately achieved. How do we do this?

1. Checking In

At the beginning of my sessions, I check in emotionally with my students. During our first session together, I explicitly teach and practice what it looks like to share when Ms. Phuong says, "What's up?" They know they can share one experience from the day using 3-4 sentences. Then, I use this information to set the tone for a session. One time, I had a student tell me his parents were in the midst of a divorce. On that day, the session leaned less on the brain and more on supporting his heart.

2. Literacy-Based Interventions

Dr. Duncan-Andrade talks about how we can get a student to the highest level of Maslow's hierarchy — the level of self-actualization. To do this, the child needs to feel that he is **relevant** and **valued**. Books are a natural (and evidence-based) way to honor backgrounds and life experiences. In our clinic, books reign. As I referenced in Chapter 2, we have even written a book on how to use books in speech therapy. Check out the book: *Literacy-Based Speech and Language Therapy Activities.* There's also more information later on in this chapter.

3. Know the Child's Superpower

My first session always centers around the child's favorite things. Is she a Pokémon zealot? Does he love Takis chips? Does he love to draw comic strips? I take this new piece of information, and I bestow the child with this Superpower. Then I find a way to incorporate it. When what you love is honored, it's amazing how hard you will work! This is a great way to speak to the heart AND work on his speech and language skills.

Let us champion the whole human being. Here's to our heart-work, SLPs. In my own heart-work, I strongly believe that gratitude is essential. So, I wrote the following words on March 12, 2018 to thank Dr. Duncan-Andrade:

*Dr. Duncan-Andrade,*

*The following heart message has been drafted dozens of times in my heart. Today, I am sending the words to you. I need you to know that your efforts have made a profound impact in my small corner of the world. By profession, I am a bilingual speech-language pathologist (SLP). I serve clients in a clinic, students in the schools, and support SLPs across our country. My human endeavors are the cumulative efforts of my parents, boat people from Vietnam. After 11 days on the South China Sea, my father (a naval captain) anchored a broken wooden boat with 55 other people in Hong Kong's harbor. My mother gave birth to me the following day. Everything I do as a professional and parent of 3 spirited offspring begins with this story. You are now a valuable part of this tale.*

*Because of the (powerful and meaningful) dialogue of my experiences (poor, immigrant, English Language Learner), I support our most vulnerable children with a fervor. After being in the field for a decade and a half, I came across your work as I tried to find research to convey to my peers the importance of the comprehensive needs of the humans we serve. For the first time, someone understood. Someone understood! You understand.*

- *You understand the nuances of equality and equity.*
- *You understand the socio-emotional needs of our human brain.*
- *You understand the social justice component we all carry.*
- *You understand the hope, the hope, the hope.*

- *You celebrate the damaged petals-- the relevant and valuable stories we all bring to our spaces.*

*I now share your heart work and your messages with my colleagues, and it's causing an important ripple in our field. It's time we begin to understand and empower through our communicative efforts. So, thank you.*

*Grateful,*
*Phuong*

You know what? He responded:

*Greetings,*
*Thank you so much for your kind words and for your service to our community. It is an honor to know that some of our work has resonated with your sacred path. I look forward to the day when we meet in person,*

*-JDA*

So now I keep this self-made visual next to my desk:

## Know Your Goals

I've seen a variety of therapy settings, and I've met a lot of kids on different campuses. One of my first questions is always, "What do you work on in speech?" I have not yet conducted the research on this; however, I ballpark that 80% of the children respond with "I don't know" or "I play games!"

Now, there are many books out there for adults on how to achieve goals. Pulitzer-prize winning reporter, Charles Duhigg, talks about the importance of developing habits. Chip and Dan Heath, authors of *Switch: Making Change When Change is Hard*, discuss limiting choices and creating small wins. Daron Roberts, author of *Call an Audible*, tells us to "stay in the deep end" and be comfortable *with the uncomfortable* to make meaningful changes. The one "given" that is stated over and over and over is that you need to first define your goal. What do you want to change? Do you want to exercise 3 times a week for at least 30 minutes? Do you want to own a house within the next 5 years? Do you want to lose 15 pounds? I am going to bet that it would be difficult to lose 15 pounds if you do not know that's what you want. For the record, you are lovely the way you are—size does not define us. Oh, bring on the tacos, bún bò huế and fried pickles, please!!

What does this have to do with speech-language pathology? Mastering a speech and language goal is harder if the student does not know he is working on it. So, start every single session with reviewing the student and client's goals. Personally, I use a chant I created several years ago. There's some brain-based magic to it, and they remember it.

If you are a visual or auditory learner, you can see Jessie showing you what this "looks like" and "sounds like" on this video: HTTPS://BILINGUISTICS.COM/SPEECHTHERAPYGOALS

I Work
(Clap, Clap)
I Work
(Clap, Clap)
I Work On:
____________________

Brain-Based Teaching and Learning

One effective way to maximize our time with clients is to utilize brain-based teaching strategies. These strategies, derived from the area of neuroscience in the 1980's, are considered brain-friendly, meaning it is the deliberate engagement of the brain when teaching. We know that lecturing and "talking at" human brains yield the lowest rate of retention (5-10%) (Sousa, 2006). In order for information to be retained, those giving the information must do something *memorable*. Recent research about the inner workings of the brain indicates that using natural brain processes will help us maximize our efforts. Research has shown that brains are capable of learning and making physiological changes throughout life—known as neuroplasticity. This means that we can *always* support positive cortical changes for our patients. Regardless of background experiences, influences of second language needs, or personality, all individuals are capable of learning. We acknowledge that all brains are unique; however, all brains have natural responses to certain events. Why is this important to us as service providers? We want to make an impact and create meaningful change during our therapy sessions, especially because these are the kids who need extra support in learning. Below are facts about the brain that impact our jobs as SLPs.

## 1. The Brain's Purpose

First, we need to acknowledge that the purpose of the brain is to serve three functions (in the following order): survival, emotional needs, cognitive learning. After the primary purpose of keeping us alive, the brain takes care of our emotional needs. As speech-language pathologists, our role is to support the communicative needs of our students. Before we can address goals and objectives, we need to make sure our clients feel safe, because stress and fear impede learning. When the amygdala is activated in the brain due to fear, the pre-frontal lobe does not function well. When students don't feel safe and comfortable, we make little progress in the areas of language, abstract thinking, thought analysis and other high-order cognitive processes.

We can combat fear by creating an empathetic, friendly environment using positive regard for our students during speech and language sessions, which improves learning. Because the brain is a social organ, the relationship you have with your client and student is important. Supportive relationships stimulate positive emotions and, as a result, increase brain neuroplasticity. Taking the time to build rapport with those you support is key for the success of your therapy interventions. Try playing a game, talking about your student's favorite movie, or incorporating the child's interests. I have learned about Minecraft, the Floss dance, Mexican elote (corn), the plot of Jeepers Creepers and the intricacies of RVs.

2. Increase Focus and Learning

Engaged brains are focused and energized (Jensen, 2013). One way to boost the engagement is to introduce physical movement. This supports increased levels of glucose and vital neurotransmitters such as serotonin, norepinephrine, and dopamine. These chemical changes improve cognitive learning and processing. A simple way to incorporate movement is to employ gestures. Learning and memory increase by many fold when gestures are incorporated (Cook et al, 2010; Stevanoni, Salmon, 2005).

3. Make Connections

Our brains work best when we make connections to personal experiences. Our thinking organs yearn for relevance. By understanding the child's background and current levels of performance, you are able to help them make connections to previous learning while reading a story. Ask the child about a time they or someone they know was in a similar situation, and teach them to transition from the narrative to their personal accounts, such as "That reminds me of a time when..." or "Speaking of..." Keep this in mind as you read about literacy in the next section.

## 4. Make It Visual

Brains appreciate visuals, a concrete representation of the content we continuously process. Visuals draw attention to important details and help organize the information that brains are processing. Words, on the other hand, take more effort to process and retain. Visual information benefits clients in three ways. It helps them a) analyze and organize information, b) integrate new knowledge, and c) think critically. Graphic organizers and story maps are two examples of effective visual tools.

## 5. Connect to Emotions

The brain pays better attention following an emotional response, and music is an effective conduit for connecting to our emotional selves. Music maximizes learning by serving as a carrier for content. For example, jazz chants, short phrases and sentences set to music and rhythm, are an effective tool for English Language Learners in school environments. Flocabulary, a web-based learning program, uses educational hip-hop music to engage students. Music is also used to energize or calm the brain to prepare for ideal learning.

## Strategies for Brain Engagement

Before Interventions

- Review previous session.
- Explicitly talk about the student's goals at every session. "You work (clap, clap), you work (clap, clap), you work on saying S sounds!"
- Check in with how the student is feeling.
- Tap into the child's prior knowledge regarding the day's theme or speech and language objective.
- Incorporate the patient's interests.

During Interventions

- Incorporate movement
- Incorporate music
- Create jazz chants
- Maintain a positive environment
- Decrease stressors
- Use visual organizers

After Interventions

- Review day's activities
- Foreshadow next session

Here is an account of a session I had:

*"It's 9:28 a.m., and I am quickly walking toward the first-grade hallway to pick up my 4 students. I have one student working on his initial /r/ sound, two students working on answering questions and story retell, and my last student is a child who stutters. The students line up, and we walk down the hall together. 'Okay, friends, why do you come to speech again?' Quickly, one child raises her hand. I nod, and she starts her goals rap, "I-work (clap, clap). I-work (clap, clap). I-work-on-tell-ing-stor-ies!" As she happily states her speech and language goals, her peers clap in beat to her chant.*

*The other three students tell me their goals, and we arrive in the classroom. We sit down, and I pull out my phone and begin playing hip-hop beats. All four pairs of hands start to move to the motivating beat, heads start to move up and down and side to side and shoulders begin to shimmy. On the designated beat, all four students start the story grammar rap, 'Char-ac-ters-are-the-peo-ple-in-a-stor-y, in-a-stor-yyyy!'*

*The most beautiful part is that just two sessions ago, these students did not know their goals or the parts of a story. By adding movement, music and continual connections to their experiences, I am able to get the most out of my speech therapy. The best part? I get awesome progress, and my students are having a blast while working on their goals. It's a win-win, for sure."*

## Literacy-Based Interventions

Books have been my constant comfort. Truth be told, I credit this to LaVar Burton and the magic of the PBS show Reading Rainbow. For many years, I recall only having a few books within our small home. First, we had Richard Scary's vocabulary book, Best Word Book Ever. Má and I would sit on our bed and study together. I was six at the time. Then, in first grade, Bá purchased Laura Ingalls Wilder's set of books for me. He particularly appreciated the value of getting nine books for such a good price. I read the series over and over and over again. There is surely comfort in hearing of another young girl's hardships.

How do we best support our diverse caseloads in the arena of intervention to maximize our efforts? This portion of the book will address the evidence-based research and provide strategies for using literacy-based interventions to support the cognitive, socio-emotional and social justice needs of our clients. Research shows that literacy-based intervention is effective. We know that reading and books provide big bang for our SLP-time-buck. I want to take the topic of literacy-based intervention and add some more layers to it. So stick with me, SLPs.

First, let's bring back Dr. Duncan Andrade. He teaches the importance of the *relationship* that exists between you and the individual you serve. He speaks of the value of love and belonging. This rapport then builds *trust*.

Additionally, Dr. Duncan-Andrade builds on his educational research by discussing the three areas that must be fulfilled to meet the comprehensive needs of a person: academic rigor, socio-emotional needs, and social justice.

For us, academic rigor equates to the speech and language learning that needs to take place. Socio-emotional needs, previously discussed, are served through the relationship building between the student/client and the SLP. Lastly, we will discuss the social justice component. Social justice is defined as "a concept of fair and just relations between the individual and society. This is measured by the explicit and tacit terms for the distribution of wealth, opportunities for personal activity, and social privileges" (Hornby, Deuter, Turnbull, & Bradbury, 2015). Each student brings his/her narrative within society into the therapy room. Factors contributing to the social justice component include, but are not limited to, skin color, socio-economic status, language use, experience, and perspective. Dr. Duncan-Andrade states that successful teaching is a combination of academic rigor *and* a pedagogy focused on social justice (Duncan-Andrade, 2009). This is *honoring, valuing* and *giving meaning* to the student's life path.

Okay, let's break down this meaty content. I have already told you my favorite story of how I grew up as an immigrant living in a bi-cultural world. When you strip away my profession, my possessions, my (allegedly offbeat) humor and my education, the core of who I am boils down to my experiences as an Asian-American girl growing up in rural Wylie, Texas. I had a lovely childhood in a loving home. I am also a person who witnessed racial discrimination, served as the interpreter for my parents beginning in the first grade, and resided in a two-bedroom home on wheels. Now, as little-Phuong went to school, I experienced educators who honored my narrative and, whether intuitively or purposely, placed value on my personal story. Miss Liz Berry asked about my family's journey. Mrs. Beverly Minahan praised my hand-crafted Valentines when Kindergarten-me realized that I only made enough for 6 of my 60 classmates—I had no idea what Valentine's Day was. SLPs, we have to understand that the story that exists within each person is important.

Next, it's going back to what the brain needs. In the Brain-Based section of this book, we talked about how brains learn best when information is repetitive, applied to background experience, connect to us emotionally, and presented thematically. So, let's recap:

- Relationships and rapport building
  - Trust is earned
  - Honor the personal narrative
- Incorporate brain-based learning
- Use literacy-based approaches to maximize learning

Literacy-based interventions provide a natural, all-encompassing method of addressing language and speech goals, building relationships through stories, and honoring the social justice components of the patient. Here are six considerations when incorporating literacy into your speech-language therapy sessions:

1. Connect to experience

Robert Marzano, an educational researcher, states, "What students already know about the content is one of the strongest indicators of how well they will learn new information relative to the content." In other words, children gain content more easily when they have knowledge of the information being taught. You can bridge this gap by taking the time to connect the book to their lives. Two easy ways to make that connection include using the front cover illustration to ask questions such as, "Have you ever been in a treehouse?" Also, try showing short videos about the content. "Let's watch this video about a farmer."

2. Represent diverse narratives

Select books representing diverse narratives. Currently, I'm using *Julián is a Mermaid*, a wordless book by Jessica Love, with my school-aged clients. For my older students, I use Ellen Oh's *Flying Lessons*, a compilation of short stories by diverse authors.

3. Value home language

Support families in reading and speaking their native language at home. We often hear, "Am I confusing my child by speaking and reading to him in my native language?" The answer is a resounding no! The truth is that the number of languages a child speaks does not contribute to communication deficits. What is important is the complexity of the language used. If we ask parents and caregivers to interact in a language undeveloped and foreign to them, the child's communication will not grow sufficiently. However, if parents/caregivers provide a great language model, the linguistic abilities gained will transfer from one language to the other. For more research-packed content on why parents should speak their native language, please read our blog post at: HTTPS://BILINGUISTICS.COM/SHOULD-I-STOP-SPEAKING-MY-NATIVE-LANGUAGE-WITH-MY-CHILDREN/

Do you want more information on using books in speech-language therapy sessions? As I've mentioned before, my dear friend and colleague, Scott Prath and I wrote a book on it. Our *Literacy-Based Speech and Language Therapy Activities* (2017) provides step-by-step strategies, templates, lists of books (for preschool through adulthood), information for alignment to general-education curricula, and goal recommendations organized by age, theme, and communication skill needs (e.g., vocabulary, syntax.)

4. The brain likes stories

I want to share one more thing about using the power of stories in our interventions. Lead your first session with a personal story. I have already talked about the importance of building relationships and rapport when we do our speechy work. Here is why *the first story*, as discussed by Dr. Seán Arthurs of Harvard, earns speech and language success for our clients:

When someone hears a story, many parts of the brain (not just the language centers) are activated (Widrich, 2012). This builds engagement. So, know that using a story is an evidence-based practice for activating the brain. Jeremy Hsu tells us that stories are a series of cause-and-effects, and the brain thrives on this. From an evolutionary perspective, this has kept us safe from predators.

5. Stories connect us as humans

When we hear a story, it naturally gives the opportunity to connect to our own personal narratives (Danesi & Danesi, 2018). I often begin my first session by telling my family's refugee story. Amazingly, my clients and students have easily found ways to connect. "Ms. Phuong, my parents grew up in another place, too! Cô Phương, I've been on a boat. Cô Phương, my mom had a baby, too!"

6. Narratives build trust

When a story is shared, trust is earned. When stories are exchanged, even more trust is earned (Simmons, 2015). And when trust is earned, communication increases (Covey, 2014).

## The Big Four: Brain, Heart, Effort, FUN.

We have talked about leading all sessions with a review of goals. "I work, I work, I work on SLPing!" The end of my sessions are focused on our *cumulative* efforts. We recite a chant that honors the brain, the heart, the effort and the fun. Here is how it's done:

Ms. Phuong: Put your hands on your head.
Scholars: (Put their hands on their heads.)

Ms. Phuong: Now say, "I'm smart!"
Scholars: I'm SMART!
Ms. Phuong: Put your hands over your heart.
Scholars: (Put their hands on their hearts.)
Ms. Phuong: Now say, "I've got a kind heart."
Scholars: I've got a KIND HEART!
Ms. Phuong: Now, raise one fist into the air.
Scholars: (Raise one arm.)
Ms. Phuong: Now say, "I worked hard!"
Scholars: I WORKED HARD!
Ms. Phuong: Raise your other fist into the air.
Scholars: (Have both arms raised now.)
Ms. Phuong: Now say, "I had fun!"
Scholars: I HAD FUN!
Ms. Phuong: "Now, clap your hands together!"
Ms. Phuong: (with arms raised, clap twice)
Scholars: (with arms raised, clap twice)
Ms. Phuong: I can't wait to see you next time, scholars!

Again, for my visual learners, there is a video showing you how it's done: HTTPS://BILINGUISTICS.COM/GROWING-STUDENT-SELF-CONFIDENCE

I'M SMART.
I'VE GOT A KIND ♥.
I WORK HARD.
I HAVE FUN.

The Human I Support

I want to conclude this chapter with a tale. A few months ago I spoke with John, a student from the University of Virginia taking an introductory course in Communicative Disorders. He asked questions about being a speech-language pathologist, and I answered them. His final question addressed the one lesson that has made the most impact on my career as a speech-language pathologist. I would like to share this lesson through a story about my Nicholas.

I have been seeing Nicholas since 2014. He is 10-years-old, loves the Grossery Gang and telling creative, odd, or humorous stories about sneaky characters. I've been seeing him individually and in a social skills group 1-2 times a week to work on expressive language and social-pragmatic skills.

Yesterday afternoon, I was going to share that it was time for Nicholas to graduate from speech-language therapy. He came into my room and said, "I'm feeling silly today! My teacher walked out of my class, and the kids were CRAZY!" When he asked about me, I lied. "I'm feeling pretty good today. I had a really nice Thanksgiving."

In all honesty, my feelings about graduation are typically mixed. I'm a proud SLP, and I love being a speech-language pathologist. I am also going to miss this human being that I have witnessed growing and changing for our last four rotations around the sun.

Nicholas learns best with visuals. So I pulled out a piece of paper, and I asked him what we work on in speech. We always start the session by reviewing his goals. I asked him to draw a "0-10" scale for his two goals: telling a story and having a conversation. "Nicholas, I want you to give yourself a score for 'telling a story' and 'having a conversation' for 2018 and for the first time you saw me in speech." He quickly did the math and said he was 6 years old. He was in the first grade, and the year was 2014 for our initial session.

The self-ratings? In the arena of narrative skills, he gave himself a "4" in 2014 and an "8" for his current skills in 2018. Regarding his conversational abilities, he gave himself a "3" in 2014 and a "9" for his current day performance. He recognized his own growth, and my data aligns perfectly to his personal assessment. I then took out a yellow marker and highlighted ratings 8-10. "Nicholas, do you know what it means when you are able to tell a story and have a conversation on this yellow part of the scale?" He scooted back in his chair and flatly said, "What?" I told him it was time to graduate, and he responded with a firm, "No." I present:

Exhibit A:

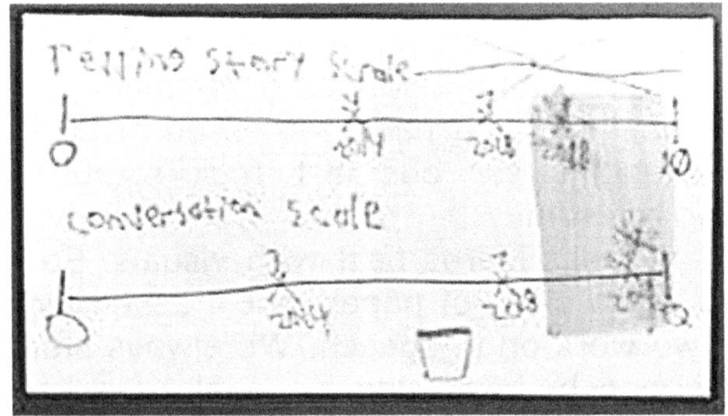


I acknowledged his efforts, expressed my pride for his earned skills and showed a plan for the remaining sessions (including a final celebratory session). My keen SLP observational skills inferred from his non-verbal language that he was *not* invested in my words.

Then he proceeded to use the skills we have been working and working and working on for the last four years to self-advocate. Here was his organized, powerful response:

1. "Theo* is in the 6th grade, and he still gets to come see you. I'm just in the 5th grade."
2. "You need to teach me *harder* things. I need to learn *harder* things."
3. "I was wrong! I'm only a "7" in "having a conversation" and "telling a story!" He then proceeded to cross out his initial answer on the rating scales. "See?! We have more work to do."
4. "You did not convince me."

Oh, how my heart swelled and ached. Here's to being an SLP. (*Name has been changed.)

You see, the story of Nicholas speaks to the relationships we have with the humans we serve. Nicholas no longer requires my support as a speech-language pathologist. It's not about "telling a story" and "having a conversation" anymore. His continued needs speak to the relationship we have built and the meaningful connections we have made.

So, I responded to the student from Virginia who was interviewing me:

"John, when I graduated from UW-Madison, I knew a lot of things. I studied hard, and I used that knowledge. Over time, I realized that **the relationship and rapport and connection made a difference**. My knowledge about speech-language pathology was only part of my work. Now, a decade and a half later, I invest in the people. I care deeply for them and, from there, we tackle the communication goals--together."

You see, dear SLPs, we get into this profession to be near people needing communication support. It's an honor to serve in that capacity, and our work is important. From my small world, though, the gains are not only made by our students. We change. As the SLP, I am forever changed by each valuable human being I serve. We gain so much from (valuable, relevant, important) them.

Exhibit B:

Danesi, M., & Danesi, M. (2018). Now, You Tell Me About Yourself: Why Do We Tell Stories? Of Cigarettes, High Heels, and Other Interesting Things: An Introduction to Semiotics, 121-144.

Widrich, L. (2012). The science of storytelling: Why telling a story is the most powerful way to activate our brains. Lifehacker. com.

# Chapter 5. Family-Centered Practice

*It's okay to take the time to build relationships and make connections. It's okay to value your humanity, SLP.*

## My Family

In the spring of 2000, as a junior at The University of Texas at Austin, my sister Kim called. She's the pragmatic one, and her words were concise. I pieced together her sentences. "Má has cancer. Her co-workers called me because she wore two different shoes to work, and she wasn't making sense. It spread to her brain. The tumor is the size of a golf ball. The surgery is this Thursday. Dr. White said that it started in her lower right lung." I hung up the phone. This was a Tuesday, my non-smoking mother has cancer in her brain and lung, and I knew that I would need to drop out of the run-off race as the University's Vice-Presidential candidate for the student body. Family reigns, and it was time to center my efforts on the woman who brought me earthside.

For the next six months, I would spend my weeks maintaining my GPA, driving the four hours (each way) between Austin and Wylie each weekend and devouring content about chemotherapy, radiation and comfy headwear for Má. With the reality of my familial needs, I was confident that I would stay in Texas for graduate school. The University of Texas at Dallas had the Callier Center, and I could live at home. The University of Texas at Austin had familiarity, my friends, and Jeremy Palafox, the kindest soul who made my heart beat a bit faster each time I saw him. And, based on experience, I knew I was only a long drive away from my mother.

Autumn arrived, and life granted me a gold nugget in the form of a full scholarship from The University of Wisconsin at Madison. I had applied to Wisconsin for kicks. It was the top ranked graduate program that year, and I did it all for ego. "Má, let's see if I can get in?!" It was not supposed to be an option. I was the daughter of a woman with cancer, and I needed to stay close. I called my mother when I received the email from Dr. Gary Weismer with this new, complicated piece of information. The pregnant woman who made the choice to step onto a wooden boat that floated into the South China Sea made my choice. She was in remission, and Whitewater, Wisconsin was our first home as refugees and it was time for me to go back. So that summer, I packed up my two-door Accord and began my drive to Madison, Wisconsin.

## John's Family

It was 2001, and there I was deep in the trenches of my first Wisconsin winter and the more challenging task of graduate school. Somewhere between reading about Brown's morphemes and researching effective ways to wear a scarf, I met John and his family. During graduate school, I worked for the Wisconsin Early Autism Project providing pivotal response treatment and discrete trial training. For two years, I spent several days a week working with this 10-year-old child in his home on his communication needs. I had left my own family to pursue my profession. I had no idea that my Wisconsin family would be so instrumental in my role as a speech-language-pathologist-to-be. Oh, the human lessons I would be gifted within the walls of their home.

Sure, I taught John communication strategies and listened to his knowledge about horses. More importantly, however, I was able to exist alongside the family—I listened to his mom, Anne, talk about the grown-up version of John and his future needs. I witnessed Caitlin advocate for her brother. I stood at the doorway on my last day and watched Michael wipe away tears as he thanked me for being a part of his son's life.

As I drove back to Texas later that spring, I vowed to always connect with my families. As speech-language pathologists, we know parent involvement supports progress.

## Research on Family-Centered Practice

I want to go back to the three components of Evidence-Based Practice I discussed in Chapter 2. The three parts include:

1. Research
2. SLP opinion/experience
3. Client/student/family perspective

Remember, adhering to the philosophies of family-centered practice is one-third of addressing evidence-based practices. The National Center for Family Centered Practice through the University of Iowa defines the key components of family-centered practice to include:

- Engaging with family members to understand their lives, goals, strengths, and challenges and developing a relationship between family and practitioner
- Working with the family to set goals, strengthen capacity, and make decisions
- Providing individualized, culturally responsive, and evidence-based interventions for each family

Per ASHA, "audiologists and SLPs recognize the essential role that families play in all aspects of service, from assessment through treatment, and the role that families and individuals play as **key decision makers**, recognized for their knowledge and skills. Families are considered from a

**lifespan perspective** and may include parents, guardians, siblings, spouses and caregivers." This part, to me, is KEY. Our parents are thinking of their child in all life stages, and this is important. Recently, I was speaking to a mother with a toddler diagnosed with a rare syndrome caused by a genetic variation. As a speech-language pathologist, my initial thoughts center, the child's ability to follow directions and the words he may be saying. The mother, however, was thinking, "Will he be able to learn? What will happen when my husband and I are no longer here? Will his big brother be responsible for taking care of him as an adult? Did I cause this?" Our families are in this for their children's entire lives, and that is a significant responsibility. The scope of this responsibility, in turn, has given them a seat at the decision-making table. Family-centered practice also results in our families being more knowledgeable, increased quality of life for the client, and increased satisfaction in care and services (Park, M., Lee, M., Jeong, H., Jeong, M., & Go, Y., 2018).

In reality, however, it's challenging to make this connection for many complex reasons. You don't always get the luxury of home-based treatment. You may not share the same native language. You call and the number is disconnected.

We need to be okay with a variety of family participation levels without judgment and with out-of-the-box thinking. So, let's talk about effective strategies for connecting with families:

## Time for trust

Stephen Covey, author of books such as, *The 7 Habits of Highly Effective People*, says that trust is the most essential ingredient for communication. Take the time to build the relationship with the child and family. A connection with the child contributes to his communication efforts. It also earns the family's trust, which goes a long way.

Recently, I did a keynote address for a parent conference put on by a nearby school district. On this occasion, a parent of one of my clients, Nicholas, whom I mentioned in Chapter 4, was in attendance. At the end of my chat, I let the audience know that Maria, Nicholas' mother, was in the audience. After five years of being a part of Team Nicholas, Maria and I are comfortable in our relationship with one another.

We have also both been witness to Nicholas' phenomenal success. I spoke honestly to the parents, and I stated that, early on, I had not yet earned Maria's trust. In that moment, her hand shot up, and she said, "Ms. Phuong, I need to say something to everyone." Trust goes both ways, and I gestured for her to continue speaking to the room full of parents and special education educators. "You are right. I did not trust you but Nicholas trusted you, and that mattered." Let us earn our family's trust.

## Functional Family Priorities

Ask the family what's important to them. A five-minute conversation builds trust and rapport, gives insight on daily living needs, and initiates a relationship. As previously stated in Chapter 2, using an open-ended comment, such as, "Tell me about what worries you," gives families an opportunity to share their short-term and long-term concerns. For those who speak another language, find an interpreter through local organizations, team members who speak the same language, or family members who can interpret.

Families also appreciate seeing direct outcomes of speech-language treatment. This happens more often when goals and objectives affect the child's daily functional living. Families want to support their child's efforts (e.g., mealtime, play time, bath time). By communicating with the family, you can focus on what will yield the most outcomes. In terms of goal-writing, SLPs are guided to write SMART goals:

**S**pecific
**M**easurable
**A**ttainable
**R**elevant
**T**ime Bound

Know that the "specific" and "relevant" goals relate to the client/student's individualized needs. The most functional of goals typically address health, safety and independence within everyday, functional environments.

For a parent-friendly resource to use within daily, functional activities, please read

Bilinguistics' *Routines- Based Early Intervention Guidebook*.

Communication Creativity:

Use various forms and modes of communication. By showing what a technique "looks like" and "sounds like," families at home can recreate the same communicative opportunities. Additionally, for some families, communicating via email or text is more feasible than oral communication. I find this true, at times, when I work with families from diverse backgrounds. With an email or text, families have time to translate the message. Also, I find using opportunities such as drop-off and pick-up time are effective for communicating with families.

Prioritize Pictures:

I also send pictures—via email and text—showing what the child achieved recently. A picture says so much. Even better, you can send a short video of a strategy from the session. This is another way to show a parent what a strategy "looks like" and "sounds like," and I feel that it helps clients take an important step toward generalization.

Positivity, Please:

As SLPs we have a lot to say, but families need to know you see the good in their loved ones. So when you connect with them, share what went well. Parents often tell me they never received a positive phone call before mine. This doesn't need to be the norm. Positivity surely increases trust, which in turn, boosts communication.

Rightfully Resourceful:

Even after trying all of these strategies, it's OK if a caregiver is unable or unwilling to participate. Your efforts at the school, hospital, or clinic will make a difference. As SLPs, we are MacGyvers—we can make great things happen with the available tools.

Sammy's Story

I want to rewind a bit. Earlier in this chapter, I talked about dropping out of a student government campaign during my time on the 40 acres at UT-Austin. It was during this time that I met an enthusiastic freshman by the name of Nada Antoun. Our initial relationship began with a collegiate campaign and snack consumption while making posters. Such tasks build meaningful friendships, and we continued to stay in each other's lives. Nada, on a college budget, visited me in Wisconsin during Thanksgiving so I would not be alone. We then became roommates while I pursued my one semester of my doctoral program. During my mother's funeral, I saw her kind eyes in the crowd. Then, in November of 2015, Nada brought her son Sammy in for a speech-language evaluation. He had just turned two years old, and he was not talking. I completed the report, and he received the diagnosis of *F80.1 Expressive Language Disorder*. With family-centered practice in mind, I would like to share our story.

Nada's Story:

*Our speech therapy journey began like that of many other families. We trusted our intuition and had our 2-year-old son Sammy evaluated for a speech delay, and he qualified. After months of slow progress, we had a candid conversation with our SLP about a motor planning disorder. Soon thereafter, Sammy was diagnosed with Childhood Apraxia of Speech. This diagnosis was heartbreaking and terrifying-- after all, everyone kept saying that boys talk later and he just needed a little coaching. There were so many overwhelming feelings. Initially, I worried about him, his heart. Would he be mocked? Would he have friends? Could the adult version of our sweet Sammy be confident and successful despite this uncomfortable and unfamiliar place? We immediately decided to make speech therapy our family's priority. Sammy and Phuong met 3x weekly, and the work continued beyond the walls of our therapy sessions. We worked on drills while in the car, during meals and while reading at bedtime. Next, we built Sammy's village among our family, preschool, and even gymnastics coaches. Collectively, we believed in him and supported his goals. Today, Sammy is one sound away from graduating from speech. Speech therapy changed our lives and I'm no longer scared for him. I know we've given him the tools to be an effective and expressive communicator despite the adversity and uncertainty of a speech disorder.*

Phuong's Story:

*I met Sammy in 2013 a few months after his birth. His mother was a close friend. Two years later, he walked into my clinic, and I became his speech-language pathologist. I'll be honest—the shift in our relationship made me nervous. As an SLP, my priorities were to 1) develop trust and rapport with the family as their clinician and 2) use evidence-based practices to make progress as quickly as possible. After months of therapy and delayed progress, I realized that the initial diagnosis of expressive language disorder was incorrect. Sammy was a child with CAS, and I required more knowledge. Now, I needed to add an additional task to my efforts—gain more education regarding his diagnosis. I was transparent with his parents, and then I quickly reached out to peers with expertise with CAS. I made changes in my therapy, and Sammy soared. In November of 2017, he walked into my therapy room and said, "Phuong, I'm ready to work on my speech sounds today!" My SLP brain heard all of his speech sounds, and my human heart was grateful for the opportunity to be an integral part of his communication journey.*

*Nada and I shared our story, Considerations for the Family/SLP Relationship, with the American Speech-Language-Hearing Association. In this piece, we transparently discuss ways in which to* ***manage expectations*** *when working alongside families. In all endeavors, unexpected events happen. In this case, when progress was not made, I was* *transparent with the family. I reported the data, recounted the steps taken to obtain more knowledge about CAS (e.g., reaching out to experts, reading articles), and developed an individualized plan for Sammy and his family. And, finally, we spoke of the value of collaboration. We are surely* ***better when working together*** *for our families, surviving together. Sammy's communication success has been astounding, and it could not have been done without our collective efforts. Here's to his accomplishments and his collective village.*

The Grown-Up Version of our Students and Clients

Sammy just celebrated his fifth birthday, and we have some time before he becomes an adult. But I want to talk about the future. I think a great deal about the students and clients we serve. Specifically, I give heart-thought to the grown-up versions of our students and clients. About six years ago, I was asked to come to a fifth-grade graduation where one of my former students, a graduating high school senior, was the keynote speaker. It had been almost ten years since I was her SLP. And remember John? He is now in his twenties. Collectively, these two young adults are now doing the following:

1. Holding conversations
2. Advocating for themselves
3. Working
4. Honoring personal interests
5. Meaningfully participating in their communities

Their stories have made an impact on me. More importantly, it reminds me of the scope of our practice. Honestly, when I was working on their social skills, I thought about them as forever being in 4th grade. At most, I thought about the next campus they would be attending. Their parents, however, always spoke in terms of life-long need. John's mom, Anne, always advocated for giving him skills that would make a difference in his future job. And, now, with John's heart desires and his mother's tenacious spirit, they will reach their goal.

These stories also remind me of the opportunities we have to be a part of the families' lives. I know the work we do in our field makes a difference. However, at times, it is hard to see the fruits of our labor. The families are the ones who are able to show us the full scope of our work. I am reminded to focus on the student's collective life and their families' lifespan needs.

Years ago, I recall sitting in an Individualized Education Plan (IEP) meeting for one of my students. Members around the table included parents, service providers (SLP, Occupational Therapist, Adaptive PE), teachers, district leads and administrators. The child was in the fourth grade, and parents were wanting us to add an objective related to using a smartphone application for the child to independently travel from one location to another. There was discussion relating to the "educational need" component of the requested goal. As I look back on this meeting, I reflect on *why* the parents made this request.

They were looking at the big picture for their son. They wanted him to start working on *functional* skills that would contribute to his quality of life as an adult. To be honest, they were on the right track.

Let's talk about transitioning and futures planning and how that relates to speech and language goals.

What's this all about?

- It's about creating a meaningful adult life for the child–right now.
- It's about giving the child self-determination skills, the skills needed to direct one's own life and needs.

And truth be told, it's amazing what happens when we let our children reach their fullest potential by giving them the space to make mistakes, believe in their own abilities and become independent.

In 2003, after two years of being a part of John's family, it was time for me to head back to the Lone Star State. My last project with John was meaningful. John loved to draw, and he drew a picture of what mattered to him most–his family. With support, he found his own words to thank his mom and dad. I did not just "work with John." I spent time with him and learned to understand the needs of those most important to him. With all team members on board, we were able to collectively support John and each other. This picture has hung in every home the family has lived in and it serves as a reminder that communication, *a life need*, is best addressed with all hearts in mind. Let's take the time to think of the grown-up versions of our clients. It's worth the time.

Anne, John's mother, sent me this email not too long ago. It's been almost 18 years since I first met the family.

*It will be a beautiful but chilly day here, John is happy to see the lower temps. As he says, "I'm a winter man." He sports a beard from October 1st to April 1st. It helps to keep his face warm when he is at work. He is still a very "by the calendar" guy.*

*John never complains about going to work. I think it is one place **he feels** calm and successful. He works at 2 stables now. Caring for the horses is definitely a life* *career for him, his choice. The horses do not ask him to participate in a conversation, their actions say it all. He has always been and will always be a visual learner. He observes the horse and can see what it needs. John's knowledge of how to care for these wonderful animals* ***amazes me****.*

*I never searched out his* ***next "angel" or life's guidance coach****, thankfully one has always been there. First with the ABA therapists, or as John has said "my workers," because 24 years ago he had to work with them to gain communication skills. He did not realize they were giving him the gift/ability of expressing his wants, needs and desires.*

*Gretchen is his employment support person, but she is* ***so much more****. John has said that she is his best friend. She has taken the* ***time*** *to observe him and find the best way to teach-communicate the tasks that need to be done at the stables and to care for the horses. John has been able to generalize those skills to other tasks not at the stable. Big step checked off the ABA list--****generalization of skills****. That one I didn't think would ever happen. He has turned into the best handyman around the house. I love it!*

As I read Anne's words, important details stand out to me as a speech-language pathologist. She talks about how he feels. This is important. She talks about the next "angel" or "life coach." I see that she did not specifically name a profession. I have come to realize that speech-language pathology is what I do, and it's important.

Notwithstanding, families are looking for "that person" to root for their child—someone who cares and someone who gives time. The way in which I impact the child (communication in this case) is secondary to the sentiments in which I convey my message to the child. Last, I hear Anne saying that generalization of skills were joyously unexpected. This is where we come in, SLPs. We can let our families know that change will be made, and it will get better. We can let our families know that their child is worthy of our efforts and our time. We can let our families know that we are better together.

I must also add that Anne wrote one of the most poignant strategies for speech-language pathologists:

Praise the accomplishment and immediately raise the bar.

## A Case Study

Recently, I reached out to the families I have supported in my professional career over the last two decades. Beginning with Anne to families I currently serve. I asked them two questions. First, what was your goal for speech-language therapy? Second, what are the top three qualities you want/ed in your speech-language pathologist? I could have assumed the responses to the first question. Families would want to improve their children's communication, and my assumptions were correct. Ellen said she wanted her son, Thomas, to speak more clearly and gain confidence using his voice. An wanted her son, Gòn, to acquire meaningful and spontaneous communication skills. Her immediate goal was for him to understand and express his basic needs so that his family could help and support him. Melody wanted her son, Greyson, to decrease the level of his frustration when communicating his needs with family and caregivers. I assume that you all got into this important profession to specifically support others' communication needs.

The responses to my second question, however, were enlightening. Now remember, families could give up to three characteristics or skills. Once families responded, I categorized the responses. The unexpected answers fell into four camps: SLP Brain Skills, Communication Skills, Child-Led Skills and Humanity Skills. I have each category with the families' responses below:

SLP Brain Skills

- Use evidence-based practices

Communication Skills

- Guide us in this process
- Time and access to SLP
- Provide practical strategies to apply lessons at home

Child-Led Skills

- Find success in the moment
- Praise my child's efforts and successes
- Child excited to go to speech-language therapy
- Accommodate child's learning style

Humanity Skills

- Be kind
- Connect with the child
- Be consistent
- Be engaging with both child and parent
- Raise the bar
- Be flexible and modify when needed
- Recognize individualized needs
- Look beyond difficulties
- Be committed to my child and his needs
- Be observant
- Think outside the box

As I reviewed the responses, I confirmed what I have felt deeply in my SLP gut since seeing my first client in Wisconsin—this field supersedes the basic pillars of communication sciences and disorders. In all of the responses I received, only one parent talked about evidence-based practices. Does this mean that we do not need to consider the research? The answer is an obvious "no." However, I want you to take note of how many "SLP characteristics" focused on skills outside of speech sound production, language, fluency and voice.

This is where my project got interesting. Families want someone to connect with their child and lead with their interests in mind. Families want you to communicate with them. Tell them what is happening in speech-language therapy. Fortunately, SLPs, we are in the profession of communicating. Families want you to be flexible. The word "flexible" was written on several occasions. This means changing my pre-planned activity to accommodate more child-led activities. This means giving space when my student is having big feelings and eventually letting her know that it's okay to be angry. This means listening to my student talk about his father who is in jail because it's important to his days as a 13-year-old.

I know the list of qualities written above is long and complex, and I know that our day-to-day responsibilities are already overwhelming at times. Here is what else I wholeheartedly believe, friends. When you first heard quiet whispers of joining this profession, you envisioned making an impact on someone's communication journey. You made the choice to become a speech-language pathologist. By default, you already possess the qualities desired by our families. I am simply giving you permission to prioritize them. It's okay to take the time to build relationships and make connections.

It's okay to value your humanity, SLP. All of these qualities exist alongside our SLP brains. It's what our students, clients, and families desire, and it is worthy of consideration. Sally, the grandparent to a young man with autism, said it best. She wanted an SLP with "transparent dedication and love."

This brings me to my final thoughts on family-centered practice. Families love their children. Love is defined as "an intense feeling of deep affection." This personal and individualized love can be shown in such diverse ways: working two jobs, sweet notes placed in lunch boxes, gifting their native language, asking educators/service providers questions about their child or giving tickets to see the latest musical. As someone who exists outside of the family unit, I acknowledge the spectrum of family routines, family priorities and family preservation needs.

So, this chapter will conclude with sentiments of love. With the definition of this four-letter word in mind, I will say that I have a deep affection for the human beings I am privileged to serve through speech-language pathology. Because of this immense love, I taught Chris how to use his communication device to tell his mother, San Juana, for the first time, "I love you." Because of this big love, I honor Miles* each time I hear his vocalic /r/ sound as he runs out of line to give me a hug. Because of this overwhelming love, I will program boy band and R&B songs into Eli's* dynamic device. Because of this great love, I told Benny*, typically quiet and unforthcoming, that she was an awesome green snake in the 2nd grade performance. So, on our last day of speech-language therapy, she said, "Love you, Ms. Phuong!" "Love you, too," I assuredly responded. I said this because it's the truth, and I earned her affections through my work as a speech-language pathologist. (*Names have been changed.)

Park, M., Lee, M., Jeong, H., Jeong, M., & Go, Y. (2018). Patient- and family-centered care interventions for improving the quality of health care: A review of systematic reviews. International Journal of Nursing Studies, 87, 69-83.

# Chapter 6. Serving our Diverse Populations

*We all speak the language of kindness.*

## Valentine 101

In January of 1985, I was a kindergartner at R.F. Hartman Elementary School. I carried home a note from school saying that I needed to bring Valentines to school. As the eldest child of refugees living in rural Wylie, Texas, my Bá and I made our best guesses. With the smattering of red hearts in the classroom and romantic holiday commercials shown during my dedicated viewings of *Growing Pains*, my 6-year-old brain knew that I needed to make red or pink hearts. Lots and lots of them. So, Bá drove me to a local drug store, and he paid for the ream of construction paper I carefully selected—the cheapest one.

Upon arriving at our home on wheels, I sat on the floor and began to carefully cut the hearts. My need for symmetry and perfection reigned, and each heart was absolute perfection. Once I was surrounded by a few dozen hearts, I began to glue the identical pieces together in a perfect row. My evening efforts culminated in 6 masterpieces, and I was proud of my work.

The next morning, Bá walked me into school. Down the long hallway, I saw 60 white bags hung, each with the students personalized kindergarten artistry. I saw the bag I decorated the week prior. I saw my peers stuffing each bag with small, white envelopes, and I saw that I messed up. I only had enough for 6 friends. In my Asian hands were the stupid hearts I cut out. The ache I felt was big. Nonetheless, the twinge of guilt on my father's face was bigger. The confident former naval captain who navigated 56 people and himself across the South China Sea following the fall of Vietnam looked defeated. He failed his child because he did not understand the words on the paper sent home from school. We failed.

In that moment, my favorite kindergarten teacher walked up to us. Ms. Beverly Minahan squatted down to my level, clasped her hands and said, "Phuong! Those are the most beautiful Valentine's I have ever seen! Which of your lucky friends will get one?" With the effort of one human and that one statement, my heart soared. I began to put my heART work into the bags of my six favorite peers. Becky Crane got one! Sarah Parker got one!

As I sit here more than three decades later, this story continues to resonate with the work I do as a speech-language pathologist supporting the comprehensive needs of our diverse populations. The kind sentiments of Ms. Minahan fuel my daily work. She reminds me, through my own personal narrative, that we are so very capable of serving our humans with relevancy and value.

## Spectrum of Diversity

Before diving into this chapter, let's talk about who we are talking about. In the past two decades, our work at Bilinguistics has primarily focused on differentiating between a speech/language difference (the natural nuances of learning a second language) and a speech/language disorder (demonstrating a true disorder in one's native language). Our *Difference or Disorder: Understanding Speech and Language Patterns in Culturally and Linguistically Diverse Children* (2014) resource provides information on accurately differentiating second-language influences and errors that are due to a communication disorder. While we think about serving our diverse populations, the content has typically addressed the needs of our English language learners.

With time, our field has begun the process of learning about and understanding the comprehensive scope of cultural competence. ASHA states that "cultural competence involves understanding and appropriately responding to the unique combination of cultural variables and the full range of dimensions of diversity that the professional and client/patient/family bring to interactions." What does cultural competency encompass? "Culture and cultural diversity can incorporate a variety of factors, including but not limited to age, disability, ethnicity, gender identity (encompasses gender expression), national origin (encompasses related aspects e.g., ancestry, culture, language, dialect, citizenship, and immigration status), race, religion, sex, sexual orientation, and veteran status. Linguistic diversity can accompany cultural diversity." (ASHA, 2017)

Because of my role as a bilingual speech-language pathologist and the primary responsibilities of Bilinguistics, this chapter will have a focus on individuals who are exposed to more than one language in their daily lives. However, I need to acknowledge that "serving our diverse populations" is rather multi-faceted, and each population deserves acknowledgement and consideration. What can this look like in our daily lives? Working with individuals who are transgender on their voice needs to live their most authentic lives. Recognizing and valuing the day-to-day needs of families living in low-income communities. Listening to the stories of our clients of color to better understand narratives that are potentially unfamiliar to our own paths.

I would like start with considerations for supporting our diverse populations: privilege, equality and equity. Then I will address effective strategies that yield beneficial outcomes for supporting the comprehensive emotional, social and communication needs of the people we serve.

## Understanding Privilege, Equality and Equity

The dictionary defines privilege as "a special right, advantage, or immunity granted or available only to a particular person or group of people." This word must be spoken, discussed, understood and accepted in order for us to justly provide services to our diverse populations. Why?

First, as service providers, it is valuable to understand that individuals of color, individuals who do not conform to binary gender norms and individuals living in poverty may not have access to the same rights and services as others do. Is this fair? Absolutely not. Is this the reality? It is and it needs to be acknowledged (Case & Rios, 2017). From my small corner of the world, I have witnessed a large Medicaid provider, serving our most vulnerable Texans, deny coverage for clients because "the requested service is not medically necessary because the member is bilingual (speaks two languages)." I have heard the stories of Child Protective Services being summoned to inquire about incorrectly assumed abuse for my families of color. A teacher has said to me, "Well, if that's how they act, I do not want them in my class." She was referring to the sole black student in her classroom at mid-school year.

Second, we need to differentiate between "equality" and "equity." Equality is giving each person the *same* amount and type of a service/object. Equity is ensuring that all individuals receive the amount they *need*. In the world of special education, this is merely individualizing and differentiating to the needs of each student. In lay terms, equality is every child getting two slices of pizza at a birthday party regardless of hunger, size and appetite. Equity is each child getting the amount personally desired with crust and toppings that align to dietary needs. How does this relate to speech-language pathology? It is understanding that our children of color, our children living in low-income communities, our children who do not conform to binary gender roles, and our children from homes that gift them with a native language that is not English have unique and relevant needs. It's knowing that Quang's behavioral needs require time and attention prior to addressing articulation needs. It's feeding Arundhati before working on narrative skills because she has not eaten since having the school lunch the day before. It's taking the time to talk to Kim's family because they are worried about his communication when he is an adult. And, finally, it must be acknowledged that equality may be a goal when in school and at the clinic or hospital; however, outside of those settings, equality does not exist (Cramer, Little, & McHatton, 2018). In thinking of the students we serve, between the hours of 3:00pm and 7:15am, life does not gift equal experiences across all families. This is the truth, and understanding these certainties give us permission to support the whole child and their family.

## Being Bilingual

I like data. It comforts me to look at the numbers behind the research. I can tell you that across the U.S, one in four children attending public school speaks a language other than English at home (U.S. Census

Bureau, 2017). In California, approximately 45% of children speak a language other than English in their home, and in my state of Texas, the percentage is approximately one-third. This is our reality. Let us contrast this with our field. There are 168,604 SLPs in the United States, and 12,242 are bilingual. That means **7.2%** of SLPs are bilingual. This means that as our nation's demographics change, SLPs are confronted with the reality of providing assessments and therapy to clients who are exposed to more than one language at home. In Texas, we are lucky to have a higher percentage of bilingual SLPs.

I speak two languages. People have told me how lucky I am to be bilingual. *To be honest, it is the only life I know, and I find this skill a double-edged sword.* I learned my first language, Vietnamese, the old-fashioned way. English was introduced to me at the age of 5 on my first day of kindergarten at R.F. Hartman Elementary. I have many thoughts about being a person who communicates in two language-worlds. Now, with knowledge of our definition of EBP leading the helm and considerations for privilege, equality and equity, I would like to share considerations for supporting our uniquely diverse populations.

1. Silent Period

I am not sure I uttered more than 100 words my entire kindergarten year. I would seesaw with Becky during recess, and I just remember seeing her mouth moving and smiling. The words made no sense. The childish grin, however, spoke volumes.

When children are first immersed in a second language environment, they often experience what is referred to as "the silent period," an unwillingness or inability to communicate orally. This is a normal phenomenon, and one I surely experienced. As an SLP, I have definitely made up for the quietness in my early educational years.

2. Interpreter, I am

Starting at the age of 6, I became my parents' interpreter. I would interpret at Eckerd's, school, Richardson Square Mall when ordering an Orange Julius – wherever and whenever needed. As a child, I was resentful. As a teenager, I was annoyed. As an adult, I am grateful I was able to assist them in communicating their needs, wants, and requests. Again, I have a better understanding of why my heart chose our awesome profession.

3. Being Bilingual = Let me help

I do not have the words to describe the joy of helping Vietnamese families and children by providing them speech-language therapy in their native language. When parents walk into a meeting and see me, I see the angst leave their faces. I have been in a meeting when the mother would tightly hold my hand and tell me, "Xin giúp tôi nói chuyện." "Please help me communicate to them." I have had the parent of a fourth grader cry after the end of a meeting. She said that it was the first time in her son's academic career when she felt like someone understood her. I interpret at meetings, and

I do assessments in Vietnamese. It is a part of my job. Every time I assist a child or family, I feel like I am making my parents proud. I am able to help and give back to people who lived my parents' lives. This feels good as I reflect on my life's work.

4. The More Languages, the Merrier

Because I am bilingual, I understand, two-fold, the beauty of each individual language. One of my greatest joys is standing in a highly dense, urban area and hearing the various languages, words and dialects swimming around me. There are sounds I admire and cannot produce. There are words I am confident I understand just by the nonverbal language that accompanies them.

5. Words are Overrated

I also see how people are able to transcend the barriers of language to communicate their intent. There's a lot to be said for a smile or a helping hand. Being bilingual is more than just talk. It is my daily interactions with my dad. It is finding the perfect word to describe the mango I am eating. It is sharing a mutual experience with a chuckle. It is surely meaningful to live in two worlds, each as important as the other.

Nói chuyện với con mình bằng tiếng mẹ đẻ sẽ giúp cho các em tiến bộ trong vấn đề học vấn. Nó sẽ giúp cho các em phát triển về ngôn ngữ và giúp cho các em thấy được là văn hóa của mình được tôn trọng. Cho nên nói chuyện với con em mình bằng tiếng mẹ đẻ là điều cần thiết và có ý nghĩa.

**FAMILIES HELP THEIR CHILDREN BY SPEAKING THEIR NATIVE LANGUAGE. IT SUPPORTS THEIR OVERALL LANGUAGE GROWTH. IT ALSO HONORS THEIR CULTURE, AND THIS IS IMPORTANT.**

## Language of Kindness

Through the years, the one comment that I have heard the most from SLPs working with children whose language they do not speak is derived from a deficit model. "I don't know what to do. I don't speak their language. I don't look like them." I'll be honest. I will say that the most impactful SLPs to serve our diverse populations have one sole characteristic—they lead with compassion when working alongside children, adults, and families who share a different personal narrative. Truth be told, the ability to speak a second language is not the answer to the question of how to serve our bilingual clients and students. I want to focus on the heart of our profession. My gut tells me that it's your *why*—why you chose our meaningful work in the first place. It is because, at the root of your daily efforts, you care and you love and you champion. You are a speech-language pathologist. You empower and support the efforts of all, *regardless of language background or zip code*, to tell their meaningful stories. Now, let's get the heart of the matter.

Kindness, a noun, is defined as the quality of being friendly, generous, and considerate. Dacher Keltner, director of the Berkeley Social Interaction Laboratory, states that human evolution has gifted humans the tendency toward kindness. Again, the brain research shows that we have propensities for socializing with and caring for others. This now brings me to a quote by Dame Minoche Shafik, "In the past, jobs were about muscles. Now they're about brains, but in the future, they'll be about the heart." Dear SLPs, this is my final intervention, an IEP of sorts.

What does kindness look like? **It means taking action.** I understand that resources and funding for bilingual services may be limited. I understand that support staff may not understand the need for a bilingual evaluation. I understand that you do not want to do harm. I understand that you want to "do them justice." Here are a few small gestures that produce valuable outcomes. I acknowledge that the considerations below have been discussed earlier in this book. In this case, it is specific to serving our bilingual population. And, because I am repeating myself, consider this an accommodation to emphasize the value of the content:

Connect

Please initiate communication with the person you're supporting. Reach out to the family. Within our clinic walls, we have found interpreters through paid services, relatives, and even restaurant employees. Often, I see SLPs paralyzed because of the language barrier. Know that each step is meaningful and worthwhile.

Be Clear

Let me remind you of Dr. Brené Brown's words, "Clear is kind. Unclear is unkind." Kindness is letting our families know our expectations. First, it is reaching out. Then, it's communicating our message clearly. It is telling our clients what is going to happen in a session. Personally, I like to talk about expectations in terms of what it "looks like" and "sounds like." This is kind. Not communicating with a family because it's hard, yet, holding them accountable and blaming them for not completing homework is unkind.

## Non-Verbal Language is Crucial

We know that most of our communicative messaging is non-verbal. Dr. Albert Mehrabian, Professor Emeritus of Psychology, UCLA, states that 93% of our communication is comprised of facial expressions, tone of voice, gestures, posture, etc. So, SLPs, use this to show kindness non-verbally. In my experience, there have been many occasions where a smile (followed by a wave) has resulted in a positive start to an assessment or IEP meeting using an interpreter for a language I do not understand.

## Say Their Names

Learning how to say someone's name, with sounds that are new to your tongue, is important. Practice it, practice it some more, syllabify it, say it to yourself, say it to them. As someone with a name like Phuong Lien Palafox, I can promise you that your efforts will be well received. And, now, I'd like to talk more about the value of names.

## What's in a Name? Everything, SLPs.

Beyoncé and I have so much in common: our love for Texas, mutual respect for Sir Jay-Z, and difficult-to-pronounce names. I admit that Queen Bey (with 17.2+ million albums sold) might now be a household name. However, I'm confident that 8-year-old Beyoncé and I lived the same life.

**Stranger:** Hi, little girl. What's your name?
**Me:** Phuong
**Stranger:** What?
**Me:** Phuong
**Stranger:** Thong?
**Me:** Ph-Ph-Ph-PHUONG
**Stranger:** Well, now! I've never heard that before!
**Me:** (silence)

As an adult, I expect mispronunciations and interesting coffee cups (Exhibit A). Why am I talking about this? As a bilingual speech-language pathologist, I'm lucky. I get to work alongside people from diverse backgrounds.

Speaking and hearing another language is a gift, and I love hearing the tones and rules of many tongues. I am also privy to names that are uncommon in the United States, and this means I also hear the commentary.

Recently, I read over 500 comments made by professionals in our field who listed "funny names" of students they've served. This was hurtful and unacceptable, and I want to talk about it.

### Why Are Names Important

As someone who grew up with a name not common in the United States, I can recount numerous occasions when peers and teachers let me know I was different. You know my origin story. What you don't yet know is that my name means "going in the right direction," and this brought my parents joy and solace. I say this because all names are chosen for a personal, individualized reason and those reasons must be honored.

Names are important because they are attached to the humans we serve. A name is a child's identity, and they will hear it and say it repeatedly. We are lucky to be in a profession that provides children ways to communicate, advocate, and empower, and *this starts with their name*.

## Tips for Remembering Names

### 1. Decide to Remember

Make a conscious decision to remember the name. Take responsibility for this objective and push aside dialogue that does not yield accountability (e.g., too hard, bad memory).

2. Pay Attention

Listen for the person's name. Be deliberate about it. Listen to the syllables, the sounds, the cadence. If you forget during the time you're together, ask again. "I'm so sorry. Tell me your name again." It might also be helpful to ask how to spell it.

3. Practice

You practice a name by using, thinking, or writing it repeatedly. When you hear the name, practice saying it aloud. Then, say it quietly in your head. As you talk to the person, use their name in conversation. When you ask a question or make a request, begin by saying the name. As soon as you can, write it down phonetically (/fôŋ/).

4. Brain Associations

The brain likes connections. Use a visual or a rhyme to help you remember. As for me, I now say, "Phuong. It rhymes with Hong Kong. It's where I was born." When I met my birthing coach Siobhan (sounds like "shu-von"), I imagined her "shoving" a "Von Trapp" child up the stairs.

## Moving Forward

In February of 2014, I went into a coffee shop. Then, the moment came. "What's the name on the order?" I told him. "How do you spell that?" I told him. I received my coffee, and I left. The next day, I walked in. The same gentleman looked at me, "Good morning, Phuong." I smiled. Then, I received my coffee, and he remembered how to spell it. It was a glorious morning, and I have the proof (Exhibit B). Doc, the gentleman, made an effort and it was surely meaningful. In conclusion, SLPs, make sure our children know that their names are valued and will serve them well.

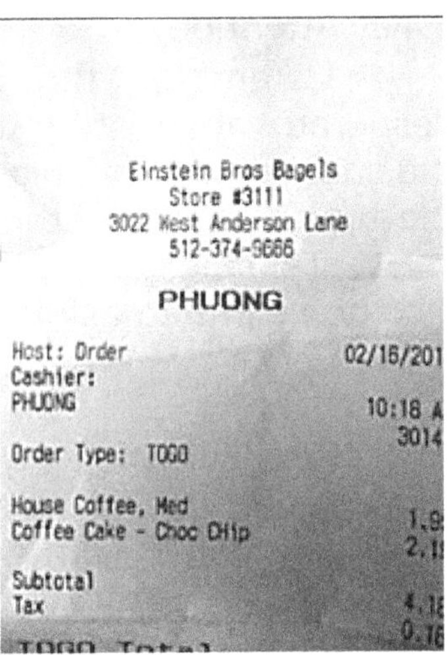


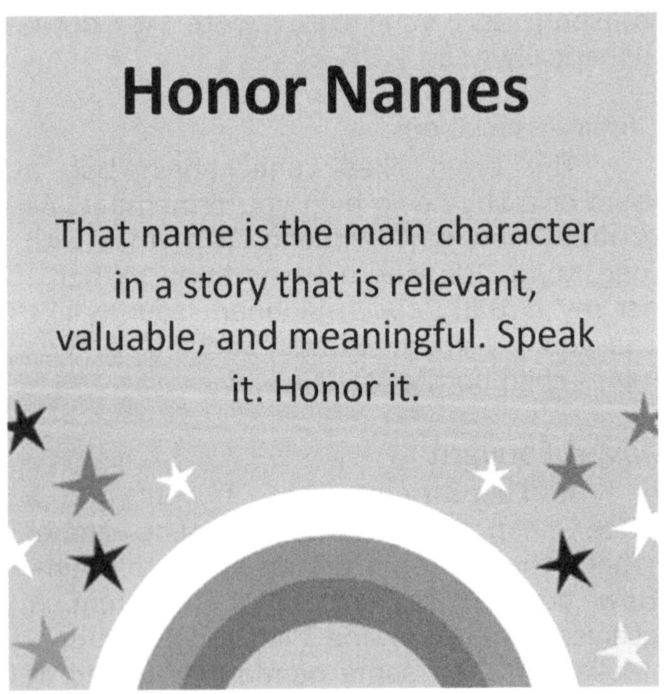

## Gratitude

It was the spring of 1997, and plans were in full swing for my upcoming high school graduation. My acceptance letter to the University of Texas to study Communication Sciences and Disorders sat in a safe place in my room, and my salutatorian speech was written. As a senior, I was able to go offsite for lunch. On that day, I forwent my fast food run and headed to an elementary campus close by. I heard that Ms. Minahan, my former kindergarten teacher, now served as the front office administrator at P.M. Akin Elementary. I drove my 1991 Geo Storm down the road, parked, and walked into the campus. And there she sat.

I quickly explained who I was in case she did not remember me. Honestly, I am not sure she did, and, truth be told, I could not tell. Twelve years after our first meeting, she stood in front of me with the same kindness and the same sincere smile. I ineloquently thanked her for how she made me feel that first year in kindergarten. She graciously accepted the gratitude, she congratulated me on my graduation, and I left.

I will say that Ms. Minahan was the first of many educators and thought-leaders who made a significant difference in my life. Ms. Liz Wells, my fourth grade teacher, read to our class each morning. She also listened to my mother's ~~broken~~ beautiful Vietnamese-influenced English telling tales of our family with loving affirmation. Ms. Thompson and Ms. David, despite my lack of noun/verb agreement, gave me the gift of writing by honoring each of my stories and articles. Dr. Jon F. Miller gave me a research job as a graduate student, gave me space to learn and grow, and allowed me to share my family's stories. Dr. Ellen Kester, founder of Bilinguistics and friend, continues to guide me in the significant work we do to serve our clients from all walks of life. You see, my list of gratitude is endless. I am thankful for the humans who honored my narrative and lifted me to the top of Maslow's hierarchy. Maslow describes this as "the full use and exploitation of talents, capabilities, potentialities... Such people seem to be fulfilling themselves and to be doing the best that they are capable of doing... They are people who have developed or are developing to the full stature of which they are capable." I am here because of the people in my life. And it is only with this support that I am sitting here in the land of Self-Actualization in which I am privileged to write this book.

As speech-language pathologists, we possess the power to be this person for those we are honored to serve. Let's lift our humans by empowering them to tell their meaningful stories.

Case, K. A., & Rios, D. (2017). Educational Interventions to Raise Awareness of White Privilege. Journal on Excellence in College Teaching, 28(1), 137-156.

Cramer, E., Little, M. E., & McHatton, P. A. (2018). Equity, Equality, and Standardization: Expanding the Conversations. Education and Urban Society, 50(5), 483-501.

# Chapter 7. I See You, SLPs

*You are living a great SLP story, and your work is significant.*

Over the last decade, I have noticed that I make people cry—convenience store owners, strangers in the parking lot, parents, students, co-workers, and many speech-language pathologists. Maybe it's because I am also a crier, and people know I'm comfortable with leaky eyeballs. I always say that tears are meaningful, and I am good at finding meaning in my day-to-day. Maybe it's because I have learned to speak truthfully with kindness, and authenticity brings on emotions? Maybe it's because I make really bad jokes? Maybe. My comedic timing is at best mediocre. I've come to the conclusion that it's because I create space for my communication partners to share wholeheartedly—without any expectations, without fixing, without judgment. And I care so much. I care *so* much about each of you, and your worth in this world needs to be honored. Oh, how I wish for it to be honored every single day.

Here's the saddest part of being on the receiving end of all those tears. SLPs, you are tired, and the work keeps getting harder. You've told me that no one is advocating for you. You've told me that you love your students, and yet you are going to quit. You've told me that you cry every day at work because you cannot get it all done. You've told me, and I see your tears. This part of the book is all about you.

## Ode to School-Based SLPs

Now, I want to talk to my school-based speech-language pathologists. I'll remind you that there are 168,604 SLPs in the U.S. A majority of you, 51.4% to be exact, work in an educational setting. For SLPs who work in health care settings (39.3%), nonresidential health care facilities (17.1%), hospitals (12.5%), residential health care facilities (9.7%) and private practice (12.1%), there is value in understanding the nuances of school-based speech-language therapy. Why? Children attend school, and supporting their communicative efforts also means supporting the efforts they make during the school day. Remember, children spend approximately 1,260 hours a year in school, and we maximize our speechy efforts when we approach communication within functional, daily activities—and this includes school.

## The Facts

When released from the throngs of graduate school, I sprinted straight toward the public sector to gleefully earn my second-rate salary. Within days, I swallowed my mother's accurate prophecy—my job as a school-based speech-language pathologist was hard. It's been a decade and a half, and I have tirelessly fought at the front lines of many public schools. Under the glow of fluorescent lights, I have witnessed moments of a school day that rattle me to my core:

1. A speech-language pathologist comes earlier than the start of the school day to have a social skills group with students—because it's the only time it can happen.
2. A speech-language pathologist changes the life of a student by giving him the confidence to speak up in class.
3. A speech-language pathologist sits outside her campus at 9pm to complete a report because she needs access to the online paperwork system that is only available on school grounds.
4. A speech-language pathologist puts on a theatrical performance for his entire elementary campus because his abilities know no limit.
5. A speech-language pathologist helps a child say, "I love you," to his mom for the first time.

There are approximately 89,000 speech-language pathologists working in the schools. According to the U.S. Department of Education, 21% of children in special education receive speech/language/fluency support. That's approximately 1.4 million children. Public schools must provide a free and appropriate public education (FAPE) to every single student.

- One out of every four children lives in poverty (that's an income of less than $24,250 for a family of four). School-based SLPs serve many of those students.
- About 1 in 68 children have been identified with autism spectrum disorder (ASD). School-based SLPs serve these students.
- Approximately 4.4 million children in the U.S. speak a language other than English in the home. These children attend public schools, and school-based SLPs serve them.

### The Noise

Now, let's talk about the noise. An SLP told me once, "I thought the not-so-good SLPs worked in the schools." Another time, an entire graduate program looked at me blankly when I asked, "Who wants to go into the schools?" Not one graduate student raised her hand. When I questioned their response, they said, "There's too much paperwork. I don't want to work alongside other professionals. I won't make as much money." I am not quite sure how this happened, but the current perspective regarding our school-based SLPs is inaccurate.

The Truth

To work in the public sector is to support all children. School-based SLPs must possess the breadth and depth to serve all children's needs. Today, I want to honor our school-based speech-language pathologists. So, school-based SLP, I want to talk to you.

Please put a bubble in your mouth and listen.

I see you.

I see you getting to school at 6:45am to make sure you are set up for the 7:30am bell.

I see you working through your lunch to hold a Lunch Bunch group for your students.

I see you spending your salary on therapy tools because the school cannot afford more.

I see you drowning in paperwork to prepare for your IEP meetings.

I see you getting down to your student's level and letting him know that he can do it.

I see you reaching out to your families from diverse backgrounds *and:* I see you speaking to them in the language of kindness.

I see you staying after school to give additional support to your students.

I see you clapping the loudest as your

students walk across that stage to get their diplomas.

I see you championing your student with unique gifts and allowing him to be the best him he can be.

I see you teaching compassion.

I see you crying with pride at your students' achievements.

I see you crying because, at times, it is too much.

I see you give, and give, and give some more.

I see them, too.

I see students learning.

I see students taking pride in their efforts.

I see students living up to the high standards you set.

I see students feeling safe when you enter their room.

I see students believing in your proud words and, eventually, in their own.

I see all of this because you are his speech-language pathologist.

I see all of this because you are her

champion.

I see all of this because you made the right choice to work in the schools.

I see your awesomeness.

I see your love.

I see your tireless effort.

I see your meaningful work.

I see your great worth.

I see the IMPACT you make.

I see you, SLP.

I see you.

I thank you.

So, all hail to our school-based SLPs! You have earned our respect, and it is time for us to back you up. We will push harder to advocate for your needs. We will ensure that you have the resources needed to support young brains. We will shout your praises louder. It's time. And, because I believe in the power of those who grace the laminate floors of our locker-lined hallways, I will be the last person standing and cheering for the greatness emerging from out of public schools.

Come join this party of almost 90,000 SLPs and their students. It's starts at

7:30am every weekday, and all are invited. Come dressed ready to work, ready to keep up and ready to make the biggest, most public, most amazing impact.

## Speech Therapy and Work-Life Balance

I have acknowledged the hard parts of our profession. Now, let's talk about the number one question I get from the readers of The Speech Therapy Blog. *How do you maintain work-life balance as an SLP?* I admit that there is an abundance of questions related to speech therapy strategies, working with English Language Learners, and service delivery models; however, once I start talking with the SLPs and SLPs-to-be, this question always comes up. Here's the one thing I've learned as a 40-year-old, full-time speech-language-pathologist, mother of three—we are all striving to find a profession that feeds the soul and allows us the opportunity to feel like we are making a meaningful difference.

## What is Work/Life Balance?

First, what exactly is work/life balance? After perusing the world wide web, I have surmised that two qualities determine success in our professional and personal lives—achievement and enjoyment. You want achievement and enjoyment in your job and in your personal life. For me, I want to fulfill my role as a partner, mother and SLP well, *and* I want to find joy as I do these things.

The problem typically arises when our professional world overtakes the time we need to dedicate to our personal lives. As a former lead to approximately 45 SLPs in a school district, I recall a conversation I had with one of my team members. Let's call her *Suzy*. It was time for our semester check-in, and Suzy reported that she stayed at school until 7pm each evening (school ended at 2:45pm) to complete all job-related tasks. She was feeling overwhelmed with her workload and did not know if she could continue as a school-based SLP for the following school year. Suzy felt like she was making a difference in the students' lives (this is her ACHIEVEMENT); however, she was losing her SLP-joy (her ENJOYMENT). And to make matters worse, the time she devoted to her job was taking away from her role as a mother to her two children. It's clear that that Suzy did not have work/life balance.

When people ask me about speech-language therapy and work-life balance, I reflect on interviews I had with SLPs who continue to make important contributions to the field, run a household and, most importantly, find joy in the profession. Let's get some perspective.

1. Honor Your Boundaries

Travis Chung, a former SLP lead in a large school district and father to a 3-year-old and infant, gives himself parameters on work and home separation. Travis does not bring his work home, and he leaves at the same time every day. Setting boundaries such as turning off phone notifications for his work email help maintain uninterrupted home time.

2. Work/Life Balance Does Not Exist Within Any Given 24 Hours

Dr. Ellen Kester, founder of Bilinguistics and mother of three, acknowledges that balance does not occur within a 24-hour time span. "I don't feel like I can have it all in one given day. It ebbs and flows." So, for Ellen, a late-night writing reports will be complemented with an afternoon attending her children's school parties. Acknowledging the realistic demands of the job along with the joys of a personal life will help set your expectations.

3. Perspective and Time Bring Clarity and Ease

Let's check back in with Travis. He also acknowledged that with more than a decade of working in the field, he is able to operate on auto-pilot more often when it comes to job-related duties. "It gets easier." And I wholeheartedly agree with him.

In Travis' words, *"Work hard. Enjoy the fun. Practice patience. Your bowl of pho will arrive before you know it."*

Early in my career, I had to put in the time to learn the processes, systems, tools, evidence-based practices, and people. This meant staying at work longer on most days to understand what I needed to do. This meant taking the time to talk to those with more experience. This meant asking for help and giving the time to those willing to help me. This meant working on the weekend to ensure that I was prepared for Monday morning. It was a humbling and memorable time.

I will also say that as I learned, I also got more organized. For example, when I used the book, *A Chair for My Mother*, I made sure to keep all of the materials organized systematically (including my go-to Storybook Intervention Template that I've used for almost a decade). That way, I could just pull out that folder for future sessions with new students and clients.

## Be all of YOU in both arenas

Here's a lesson that proved invaluable. SLP-me uses strategies with my own children, and Mom-me shares stories of my kids with my students. I love my family, and I love my job, and it's challenging to keep the two arenas separate when it comes to matters of the heart. Ellen and I both share our work with our offspring, and we bring our family stories, interests, and experiences into our therapy sessions. For instance, as you already know, I love music of the hip-hop persuasion. Coupled with some brain-based strategies, I use this form of music in my sessions. Check out the story grammar rap I created (and perfectly set to my favorite 90s rap beats):

C-c-c-characters are the people in a story!
Setting is when and where!
When and where!
Problem, hey what's wrong?
Solution, let's solve it.

You can hear more of the story grammar rap here: HTTPS://BILINGUISTICS.COM/BRAIN-BASED-LEARNING/

And, when at home, I often find myself talking to my children about the important work I do. Just the other day, my 10-year-old observed a child with communication needs in a store. When we got back in the car, he said, "Mama, you can help him! Go tell his mom!" It's amazing what happens when our work and personal lives align.

Feel Good Folder

Here is something I want you to do, SLPs. If you have not done so, create a Feel-Good folder. This brilliant idea was given to me by my awesome co-lead Tammy Qualls years ago. Keep all of the comments, notes, and feel-goods about your job in one place. Then, when you need a kind reminder about your *why*, take a journey through your Feel-Good folder. Embedded in my treasure-filled folder, I see a note from Praneit.

She thanked me for telling my family's story to her fifth-grade class during their annual Immigration Day event. I read a note from Bettina from 2012, and I am reminded that I advocated for funds to purchase materials for my SLP peers. I see a card from a parent. She thanked me for helping her son Jeremiah and their family. Jane, a colleague, wrote on a card, "I know it's a tough job that you love." Here's to the memories we are continually creating. Now keep those lovely notes and mementos in one place. As you occasionally read them you will be rewarded. Know that you are living a great SLP story, and your work is significant.

## Give Thanks

We are a part of the most fulfilling profession to exist on planet Earth, and I am pretty sure most of your "why's" have to do with the people, people, people we serve. The SLP-life can feel overwhelming–IEP meetings, evaluations, report writing, trainings, making materials, programming devices, meeting productivity percentages, etc. At times, we find ourselves losing sight of why we are in this profession. But the energetic kids, the introspective teenagers, the grieving families, the tenacious adults all make it worthwhile. Here is a message for them:

I am your SLP, and we will always have work to do. Today, I want to let you inside my daily thoughts. I have the best job in the world, and it is because of you. And, for that, I thank you.

I had a choice, and I chose well.
To give all a voice is what I yearn.
My craft, my art, is sounds and words.
I learn and work. I work, then learn.
My tools reside within my mouth.
Let's find your sssssounds—repeat, repeat!
We need your song, your big, big thoughts.
Success and pride you'll surely meet.
I see your face, your message unheard.
Let's find a mode to suit your days.
Use words, pictures, a clutch device?
I'm by your side, and we'll find a way!
Most days are long and all are hard.
To reach great goals and hope within.
Great things take effort and so much heart.
With work, success comes sauntering in.
I think of you, early morn' 'til moon up.
We will find your message and yell it with
glee
My days, with awesome-you, are grand.
With much, much, love, Your SLP.

Remember, this is a relationship. Our students are only half of the equation. As the service-providers, we are the other (equally relevant and valuable) half. So, now, I have a few words for you, SLPs:

9/12/2018

Dearest SLP,

I wanted to take a moment to say "thank you." I see you scheduling your groups (again and again). I see you running your IEP meetings with thoughtfulness for the family and student. I see you giving "high fives" and big smiles for your client finding his sounds. I see your tears, too. I know you're working so hard and there are not enough hours in the day. I see your (growing) stack of paperwork you carry from work to home. I see the list of make-up sessions due to meetings you attended.

I see all of it, and I understand why you do it. It's all for them -- our students, our clients, our families. They are worth it. And you are worthy, SLPs. Your efforts are honored, and we are grateful. Love,
Phuong

# Epilogue

I began this book by telling you my favorite tale, and I would like to conclude with a story I wrote on October 15, 2018:

I have cried an ocean in the weeks leading up to today. Exactly 40 years ago today, in 1978, my parents arrived in Hong Kong after spending 11 days on the South China Sea as Vietnamese refugees. I was born within the walls of Tsan Yuk Hospital the day following their arrival.

On this day, I shared my meaningful family tales and their impact on my profession in my keynote address for the state of Alabama. Fittingly, I then talked about the value of literacy-based interventions in the following session. Oh, the power of stories!

To say it's a full-circle moment would not be accurate. Circles repeat the same path. The privilege I have today in sharing my family's narrative is the direct result of sacrifices. Sacrifices built upon welcomed sacrifices. Today is more of a mountain moment. Má and Bá started stacking the rocks and boulders for my siblings Dan, Kim, and me. On this day, I climbed the mound carrying their stories, their hardships, and, ultimately, their dreams. Along the way, I acknowledged their efforts, and I fulfilled part of my journey—a path written in their quiet whispers before they embarked on the trip in that wooden fishing boat in 1978. For a moment, I stood at the top of our mountain and acknowledged the predestined beauty of it all.

Growing up, Má would fill the walls of our home with our awards—perfect attendance, science fair runner-up, math minute assessments. She was proud. I miss her, and I find solace in the fact that she witnessed me becoming an SLP the last year of her life. She practiced, on repeat, how to say "SPeeCH laNGuaGe paTHoLoGiST." She helped me set up my first classroom. She heard the woeful tales of my inaugural year. In the evenings, she would help me make materials for my students. It was a really good year. She died that December.

She did not, however, get to see how her stories are now shared across this country —this place in which she put all of her hopes for her child. She did not see the tears of people who have thanked me for acknowledging our narratives as immigrants. I ache knowing that the person proudest of my efforts did not have the opportunity to witness all of it. This is my truth, and I hold space for it.

Oh, how she would have clipped every presentation advertisement, blog post, and article to line the walls of her home. Every time I get to stand in front of my peers to tell our stories, I feel her tugging at me. I imagine her hanging each earned moment on stage on her motherly wall of pride.

Tears fall when a heart is too full to hold it all in, and my heart overflows today. As I embark on this 40th year of life tomorrow, I am grateful. I am grateful, and I am listening. I hear the world telling me to deeply feel and loyally follow my sacred path. So, I will continue to do so because my family, through water and land and love, earned this for me.

Photo 1: Birmingham, Alabama 2018

Photo 2: I invented a new pose. I shall call it "raising the roof" cause there ain't no ceiling in my tales.

Photo 3: Hong Kong 1978

Photo 4: Note given to me by an attendee. The front read "Phuong, I honor your story."

# My Heart Honors

These words are important. The purpose is to thank the people who have contributed to the efforts of this book. The list is long because my writing efforts are a culmination of every memory I have made. For this, I am grateful for each and every conversational exchange, hug, comment, speech-language pathology session, email received, sprinkled successes, and a multitude of failures. I will begin with my Bilinguistics family.

**Ellen Kester**, thank you for your leadership, both in mothering and in work. I first met you during the short tenure of my doctoral program. I did not obtain the degree; however, because of you, I've been given the opportunity to fulfill the goals I had initially set in 2003. Your leadership is so very honorable, and I love being witness to it.

**Scott Prath**, your life has followed a myriad of unique paths, and I feel so lucky that you chose to join our profession. This choice has gifted our field and my life. I am thankful for your kind friendship. You have stepped in and stepped up when I needed it most.

**Maritza Jacobs**, sharing stories with you is one of the most meaningful ways to start my mornings. I deeply feel that our lives have purposely intersected. Know that you were the catalyst to the initial writing of this book. For that, I will be forever grateful.

To my **SLP peers**, this book was written with each of you in mind and heart. Your continual efforts amaze me, and your worldly contributions can fuel all seven continents. You are my solace at the end of a hard day, and I will always stand beside you in solidarity as we continue our life's work.

To the **families I support**, thank you for trusting me with your child's communication journey. I am grateful for the opportunity to be a part of your daily lives. It is truly my honor. Thank you for sharing your stories and your grief. The truthful sentiments are so very valuable, and it makes me be a more impactful speech-language pathologist.

To the valuable **humans I support**, thank you for giving the world your meaningful messages. We need it, and we are better for it. Thank you for sharing your plethora of superpowers. Here's to lovely you.

To my **Jeremy**, you will always be my smartest decision. You are the first person with whom I want to share my most difficult, my most joyous, and my most mundane SLP moments. I am only able to do my work in this capacity because you are our family's sun. Your light centers our days, and your warmth settles us to sleep each evening.

To my **Zac** and **Ruby** and **Story**, thank you for reminding Mama of the significant small moments in life. Thank you for gifting me with your presence and for the honor of bringing each of you earthside. Working to provide for each of you is a gift, and I thank you for valuing my role as a speech-language pathologist.

To my sister **Kim** and my brother **Dan Lien**, thank you for walking alongside me. Both of you are the best gifts bestowed to me by our parents.

To my **bá** and **má**, words cannot convey the overwhelming swell of gratitude I have for both of you. Bá, your work ethic supersedes that of all other humans, and I am thankful you gifted me this trait. Gut also tells me that your loquacious ways have contributed to my professional skills. Má, you were always happiest talking about your children. So I made a promise to myself to work hard to see your joy. With each word written, you have been with me. I am thankful you gave me this amazing life. Look what *we* did, Má.

# References


Beed, P. L., Hawkins, E. M., and Roller, C. M. (1991). Moving learners toward independence: The power of scaffolded instruction. *The Reading Teacher*, *44*(9), 648-655.

Berninger, V. W. (2008). Defining and differentiating dysgraphia, dyslexia, and language learning disability within a working memory model. Brain, behavior, and learning in language and reading disorders, 103-134.

Brown, B. (2018). *Dare to Lead: Brave Work. Tough Conversations. Whole Hearts*. Random House.

Bruner, J. (1978). The role of dialogue in language acquisition. *The child's conception of language*, *2*(3), 241-256.

California State University. Libros Recomendados en Español/Recommended Books in English about Latinos. *Barahona Center for the study of books in Spanish for Children and Adolescence.* 2007. California State University, San Marcos <http://www.csusm.edu/csb/espanol/>.

Campbell, J. R., Kelly, D. L., Mullis, I. V., and International Association for the Evaluation of Educational Achievement. (2001). *Framework and specifications for PIRLS assessment 2001*. International Study Center.

Campbell, J. R., Kelly, D. L., Mullis, I. V. S., Martin, M. O., & Sainsbury, M. (2001). Progress International Reading Literacy Study (PIRLS). *International Association for the Evaluation of Educational Achievement (IEA), Second Edition. Chestnut Hill, MA, USA: PIRLS International Study Center.*

Carmichael, C., Callingham, R., Watson, J., & Hay, I. (2009). Factors influencing the development of middle school students' interest in statistical literacy. *Statistics Education Research Journal*, *8*(1), 62-81.

Catts, H. W., & Kamhi, A. G. (Eds.). (2005). *The connections between language and reading disabilities*. Psychology Press.

"Children's Defense Fund." *The SAGE Encyclopedia of World Poverty* (n.d.): n. pag. *Children's Defense Fund13*. Children's Defense Fund, 13 Sept. 2016. Web. 12 May 2017.

Cockerell, L. (2010). *Creating Magic: 10 Common Sense Leadership Strategies from a Life at Disney*. London: Ebury Digital.

Coppola, S. (2014). The Images Deficit in the Teaching of Writing. *The Reading Teacher*, *68*(2), 127-127.

Crowe, L. K., Norris, J. A., & Hoffman, P. R. (2000). Facilitating storybook interactions between mothers and their preschoolers with language impairment. *Communication Disorders Quarterly*, *21*(3), 131-146.

DeBaryshe, B. D. (1993). Joint picture-book reading correlates of early oral language skill. *Journal of child language*, *20*(02), 455-461.

Denham, S. A. (1998). *Emotional development in young children*. Guilford Press.

Doyle, B. G., & Bramwell, W. (2006). Promoting emergent literacy and social–emotional learning through dialogic reading. *The Reading Teacher*, *59*(6), 554-564.

Elias, M.J. (2003). Academic and social-emotional learning. Educational Practices, 11, 1-31.

Duhigg, C. (2014). *The power of habit: Why we do what we do in life and business*. Toronto: Anchor Canada.

Fey, M. E., Catts, H. W., Proctor-Williams, K., Tomblin, J. B., & Zhang, X. (2004). Oral and written story composition skills of children with language impairment. *Journal of Speech, Language, and Hearing Research*, *47*(6), 1301-1318.

Feldman, K., & Denti, L. (2004). High-access instruction: Practical strategies to increase active learning in diverse classrooms. *Focus on Exceptional Children*, *36*(7), 1.

Flocabulary.com

Frost, S. J., Mencl, W. E., Sandak, R., Moore, D. L., Rueckl, J. G., Katz, L., ... & Pugh, K. R. (2005). A functional magnetic resonance imaging study of the tradeoff between semantics and phonology in reading aloud. *Neuroreport*, *16*(6), 621-624.

Gesturing makes memories that last. Cook SW, Yip TK, Goldin-Meadow SJ Mem Lang. 2010 Nov; 63(4):465-475.

Gillam, R. B., & Pearson, N. A. (2004). TNL: Test of Narrative Language. *Austin, TX: Pro-Ed*.

Gilliver, M. L., & Byrne, B. (2009). What's in a name? Preschoolers' noun learning performance in relation to their risk for reading disability. *Reading and Writing*, *22*(6), 637-659.

Glenn, C. G., & Stein, N. L. (1980). Syntactic structures and real world themes in stories generated by children. *Urbana: University of Illinois Center for the Study of Reading*.

Gutiérrez-Clellen, V. F. (2002). Narratives in two languages: Assessing performance of bilingual children. *Linguistics and Education*, *13*(2), 175-197.

Hatch, E. (1992). *Discourse and language education*. Cambridge University Press.

Heath, C., & Heath, D. (2010). *Switch: How to change things when change is hard*. New York: Broadway Books.

Heath, S. B. (1982). What no bedtime story means: Narrative skills at home and school. *Language in society*, *11*(01), 49-76.

Hedberg, N. L., & Westby, C. E. (1993). *Analyzing storytelling skills: Theory to practice*. Communication Skill Builders.

Huennekens, M. E., & Xu, Y. (2010). Effects of a cross-linguistic storybook intervention on the second language development of two preschool English language learners. *Early Childhood Education Journal*, *38*(1), 19-26.

Hudson, J. A., Shapiro, L. R., McCabe, A., & Peterson, C. (1991). From knowing to telling: The development of children's scripts, stories, and personal narratives. *Developing narrative structure*, 89-136.

Jensen, E. (2008). *Brain-based learning: The new paradigm of teaching*. Corwin Press.

Jensen, E. (2009). Teaching with poverty in mind. *Alexandria, VA: ASCD*.

Jensen, E. (2013). Engaging students with poverty in mind. *Alexandria, VA: ASCD*.

Kester, E. (2014). *Difference or disorder?: Understanding speech and language patterns in culturally and linguistically diverse students*. Austin, TX.: Bilinguistics.

Klecan-Aker, J. S., McIngvale, G. K., & Swank, P. R. (1987). Stimulus considerations in narrative analysis of normal third grade children. *Language and speech*, *30*(1), 13-24.

Klecan-Aker, J. S., & Brueggeman, L. (1991). *The expression connection: A structured approach to teaching storytelling to school age children*. Speech Bin.

Klecan-Aker, Joan S. & Colson, Karen (2009). Criterion-Referenced Assessment for Language Organization: An Example of Evidence-Based Practice, Forum on Public Policy Online, Spr 2009

Lesaux, N. K., & Siegel, L. S. (2003). The development of reading in children who speak English as a second language. *Developmental psychology*, *39*(6), 1005.

Linan-Thompson, S., Vaughn, S., Prater, K., & Cirino, P. T. (2006). The response to intervention of English language learners at risk for reading problems. *Journal of Learning Disabilities*, *39*(5), 390-398.

Lipka, O., & Siegel, L. S. (2007). The development of reading skills in children with English as a second language. *Scientific Studies of Reading*, *11*(2), 105-131.

Melzi, G. (2000). Cultural variations in the construction of personal narratives: Central American and European American mothers' elicitation styles. *Discourse Processes*, *30*(2), 153-177.

Merritt, D. D., & Liles, B. Z. (1987). Story Grammar Ability in Children with and without Language Disorder Story Generation, Story Retelling, and Story Comprehension. *Journal of Speech, Language, and Hearing Research*, *30*(4), 539-552.

Montgomery, J. W., & Evans, J. L. (2009). Complex sentence comprehension and working memory in children with specific language impairment. *Journal of Speech,*

*Language, and Hearing Research*, *52*(2), 269-288.

Morais, J., Mousty, P., Kolinsky, R., Hulme, C., & Joshi, R. M. (1998). Reading and spelling: development and disorders. *Reading and spelling: development and disorders*.

Ninio, A., & Bruner, J. (1978). The achievement and antecedents of labelling. *Journal of child language*, *5*(01), 1-15.

Noble, K. G., Norman, M. F., & Farah, M. J. (2005). Neurocognitive correlates of socioeconomic status in kindergarten children. *Developmental science*, *8*(1), 74-87.

Parnell, M. M., Amerman, J. D., & Harting, R. D. (1986). Responses of language-disordered children to wh-questions. *Language, Speech, and Hearing Services in Schools*, *17*(2), 95-106.

Poveda, David. "La Ronda in a Spanish Kindergarten Classroom with a Cross-Cultural Comparison to Sharing Time in the USA." *Anthropology & Education Quarterly* 32.3 (2001): 301-325.

Prath, S., & Palafox, P. (2017). *Literacy-based speech and language therapy activities: Successfully use storybooks to reduce planning time, easily work in groups, and target multiple communication and academic goals*. Austin, TX: Bilinguistics.

Proctor, B. D., Semega, J. L., & Kollar, M. A. (2016). Income and poverty in the United States: 2015. Washington, DC: United States Census Bureau, September.

Rabidoux, P. C., & MacDonald, J. D. (2000). An interactive taxonomy of mothers and children during storybook interactions. *American Journal of Speech-Language Pathology*, *9*(4), 331-344.

Raz, I. S., & Bryant, P. (1990). Social background, phonological awareness and children's reading. *British Journal of Developmental Psychology*, 8(3), 209-225.

Rice, M. L., Bishop, D. V. M., & Leonard, L. B. (2000). Grammatical symptoms of specific language impairment. *Speech and language impairments in children: Causes, characteristics, intervention and outcome*, 17-34.

Roberts, D. K. (2016). *Call an audible: Let my pivot from Harvard Law to NFL coach inspire your transition*. Austin, TX: River Grove Books.

Roettger, C., Roettger, L. O., & Walugembe, F. (2007). Teaching: more than just lecturing. *Journal of University Teaching & Learning Practice*, *4*(2), 6.

Shiro, Martha Klein (1998). A discourse analysis approach to evaluate stance in Venezuelan children's narratives. *Dissertation Abstracts International: Section B: the Sciences and Engineering. Vol. 58 (8-B).*

Silliman, E. R., Bahr, R. H., Brea, M. R., Hnath-Chisolm, T., & Mahecha, N. R. (2002). Spanish and English proficiency in the linguistic encoding of mental states in narrative retellings. *Linguistics and Education*, *13*(2), 199-234.

Sinek, S., Mead, D., & Docker, P. (2017). *Find your why: A practical guide for discovering purpose for you and your team*. Penguin.

Sousa, D. A. (2006). How the brain learns? 3rd ED). Thousand Oaks, CA: Corwin Press.

Stein, N. L. (1988). The development of children's storytelling skill. In *Portions of this paper were presented at the Eleventh Annual Boston University Child Language Conference, Oct 17-19, 1986*. Oxford University Press.

Stevanoni E., Salmon K. (2005). Giving memory a hand: instructing children to gesture enhances their event recall. J. Nonverbal Behav. 29, 217–233.

Swanson, L., Fey, M., Mills, C., & Hood, L. (2005). Intervention with children who have specific language impairment. American Journal Of Speech--Language Pathology, 14 (2), 131--143. *Pathology*, *14*(2), 131-143.

Teale, W. H., & Sulzby, E. (1986). *Emergent Literacy: Writing and Reading. Writing Research: Multidisciplinary Inquiries into the Nature of Writing Series*. Ablex Publishing Corporation, 355 Chestnut St., Norwood, NJ 07648.

Tomblin, J. B., Zhang, X., Buckwalter, P., & Catts, H. (2000). The association of reading disability, behavioral disorders, and language impairment among second-grade children. *Journal of child Psychology and Psychiatry*, *41*(4), 473-482.

Treiman, R., Hulme, C., & Joshi, R. M. (1998). Beginning to spell in English. *Reading and spelling: Development and disorders*, 371-393.

Ulatowska, H. K., & Chapman, S. B. (1994). Discourse macrostructure in aphasia. *Discourse analysis and applications: Studies in adult clinical populations*, 29-46.

Van Daal, J., Verhoeven, L., & Van Balkom, H. (2007). Behaviour problems in children with language impairment. *Journal of child psychology and psychiatry*, *48*(11), 1139-1147.

Ulatowska, H. K., & Olness, G. S. (2001). Dialectal variants of verbs in narratives of African Americans with aphasia: Some methodological considerations. *Journal of Neurolinguistics*, *14*(2), 93-110.

Vygotsky, L. S. (1980). *Mind in society: The development of higher psychological processes*. Harvard university press.
Wilson, M. S., Fox, B. J., & Pascoe, J. P. (2012). Asking and Answering Questions; Theory & Research Based Intervention.
Weizman, Z. O., & Snow, C. E. (2001). Lexical output as related to children's vocabulary acquisition: Effects of sophisticated exposure and support for meaning. *Developmental psychology*, *37*(2), 265.
Westby, C. E., & Simon, C. (1991). Learning to talk, talking to learn: Oral-literate language differences. *Communication skills and classroom success*, 334-357.
Whitehurst, G. J., Adamson, L. B., & Romski, M. A. (1997). Language processes in context: Language learning in children reared in poverty. *Research on communication and language disorders: Contribution to theories of language development*, 233-266.
Zins, J. E. (2001). Examining opportunities and challenges for school-based prevention and promotion: Social and emotional learning as an exemplar. *The Journal of Primary Prevention*, *21*(4), 441-446.

Made in the USA
Coppell, TX
28 August 2024